The Misdirection of Education Policy

The Misdirection of Education Policy

Raising Questions about School Reform

Nancy Avery Dafoe

ROWMAN & LITTLEFIELD
Lanham • Boulder • New York • London

Published by Rowman & Littlefield
A wholly owned subsidiary of The Rowman & Littlefield Publishing Group, Inc.
4501 Forbes Boulevard, Suite 200, Lanham, Maryland 20706
www.rowman.com

Unit A, Whitacre Mews, 26-34 Stannary Street, London SE11 4AB

Copyright © 2016 by Nancy Avery DaFoe

All rights reserved. No part of this book may be reproduced in any form or by any electronic or mechanical means, including information storage and retrieval systems, without written permission from the publisher, except by a reviewer who may quote passages in a review.

British Library Cataloguing in Publication Information Available

Library of Congress Cataloging-in-Publication Data Available

978-1-4758-2830-6 (cloth: alk: paper)
978-1-4758-2832-0 (pbk: alk: paper)
978-1-4758-2833-7 (electronic)

♾ ™ The paper used in this publication meets the minimum requirements of American National Standard for Information Sciences Permanence of Paper for Printed Library Materials, ANSI/NISO Z39.48-1992.

Printed in the United States of America

The time has come to consider what science might give to the humanities and the humanities to science in a common search for a more solidly grounded answer than before to the great riddle of our existence.

—Edward O. Wilson, *The Meaning of Human Existence*

Contents

Foreword: Look with the Eyes of a Scientist		ix
Preface: Strangeness of Ideas		xiii
Acknowledgments		xix
Introduction: Examples and Non-Examples		xxi
1	We're Funding the Left Side of Your Brain	1
2	"If I Didn't Write in This Journal . . ."	7
3	Why Aren't Schools Run Like Businesses?	11
4	Faulty Logic, Public Discourse	19
5	Tales Told by Idiots Signifying Nothing	25
6	Why Teacher Evaluations Tied to Tests Don't Work	31
7	What Hurt	41
8	Public Education Paradigm Shifts Menu	45
9	Common Core Head First	49
10	Why Students Should Read Tolstoy and Faulkner	59
11	Consequences of Exclusionary Parameters	65
12	Education without the Humanities	73
13	What You Don't Know	77
14	Master Teachers in Every Classroom	81
15	Welcome the Subversive	85
16	Insights from the Humanities	89
17	Allow Every Teacher to Engineer Reform	93
18	*The Waste Land* Revisited	97
19	Creating Meaningful, Lasting Reform	101
20	Convergence of Poetry/Science: An Interdisciplinary Approach to Teaching and Learning	105
21	Raining Poets	113
22	The Answer Is the Question	123
Appendix A		127
Bibliography		129

About the Author of the Foreword 135
About the Author 137

Foreword

Look with the Eyes of a Scientist

What do scientists do? We ask questions. We examine carefully in order to problem solve. Nancy Dafoe's book is about the importance of asking questions at the heart of policy in education reform.

A few years ago, I sat in one of Dafoe's workshops on creating concept journals across curricula, and I found delight and surprise in the power of metaphors to "guide the mind." It was one of the first times I discovered the richness of connotative language and the associations that each comparison brings to the table. It was not only revealing but fun to create metaphors relating to chemistry, and I noted Dafoe's ease in incorporating good teaching practice in her workshop. We were all actively creating, not simply listening.

I have neither forgotten the lessons in that workshop nor the significance of writing well in my own concentrations of study. It is not enough to do good science; we must articulate our subject matter well. Without good communication, without clear, concise, and engaging language, our ideas can become lost or never find audience and/or implementation.

Imagine our world without Darwin's science fluently expressed in his seminal book *On the Origin of Species*. I recall one of my own early inspirations in chemistry—Harold McGee—and that what drew me to him initially was his book *On Food and Cooking*—how the chemistry of cooking was revealed through and by his language in a book. I was hooked on McGee's science through his cookbook. The concepts of teaching chemistry through cooking have been one of my pleasures, as well as great successes in the classroom.

In any field, we all discover inspiration—the next creative approach to engineering, to solving a problem—in myriad ways. The sources are as diverse as listening to music in a symphony orchestra, looking at the results of a "failed" experiment, or viewing a painting in the National Gallery of Art, as I have had the good fortune to experience recently as a year-long resident of Washington, DC. The connections between diverse spheres are infrequently examined, yet disclosed after we begin our exploration.

It has been well documented that our revelations often occur when we are working outside of our academic areas. If we only study science and mathematics, our science and mathematics will, indeed, be poorer for it, regardless of expertise. If we only study engineering, our ability to conceive of innovations and problem solve at the highest levels will be greatly diminished.

As a 2015–2016 Albert Einstein Distinguished Educator Fellow and STEM (science, technology, engineering, and math) teacher, I have long felt the need, as well as the urgency, to reform public education in order to help our students better prepare for a world in which we either lead or are left falling further behind. Comparing our children to those in sixty-four other, developed nations, we are—at best—average in science and reading, and at worst, below average in mathematics on the 2012 PISA, or the Program for International Student Assessment.

Discouragingly, this particular test was given after the implementation of reform legislation No Child Left Behind and Race to the Top, across political aisles and demographics. Whether reform is directed from the Federal or the state governments there appears to be much in the mandated regulations that still suggest far too simple solutions are to be applied to very complex problems. Dafoe asks us to step back and examine our reforms, analyze, and reconsider before rushing into yet another program that meets with failures.

There is clearly no dearth of evidence that indicates our students' science and mathematics' scores are not where any of us want them to be in comparison to the world's leaders in these critical areas of life and study. What we do about those numbers, however, needs better analysis and learned discussion by educators rather than politicians. Not surprisingly, there is no one-step process or no overnight fix to the many variables in the equation as to why children are unsuccessful in school. Good teachers get this, but too often policymakers seem unaware of this basic fact.

What was the public response to the poor PISA results? When the *Washington Post* printed American students' scores in 2013, one of the anonymous comments to Valerie Strauss's article called for an "end to public schooling" and the beginning of funding "only a manager class in this country."[1] Yikes. Yet we have heard those unacceptable sentiments echoed around the country, particularly by those who do not understand what is involved in learning, in teaching.

How do we make progress? Dafoe suggests we start by asking the questions that are not currently being raised. There is a mathematical symmetry to her argument in the way that we must approach algebraic problems. How do we figure out the "unknowns" in order to solve the equation?

Like Dafoe, I refuse to be an apologist for America's weak or middling scores. Our children, our students have a right to the best we can offer them, and they, in turn, have an obligation to make the most of their educational opportunities. This does not necessarily happen. Why? The reasons are multitudinous but not insurmountable, as Nancy Dafoe points out in her paradoxically funny, serious, and critically important book *The Misdirection of Education Policy*. This book should serve to continually reopen conversations we must have in order to improve our offerings for students. We need to be constantly assessing and reassessing to make meaningful progress. What could possibly be worse for education than closed discussions, closed minds?

Although Dafoe comes from a humanities background and I hail from the science and mathematics educational construct, we are on the same page: educators need to be passionately and directly involved in designing and improving their lessons for students. Teachers also need to be involved in reforming educational processes. Teachers and students need support in the reform movement. They need support in the effort to change. Those changes will likely be attached to some failures, and those failures take place at the edge where we learn, where students and teachers try, back up, turn a corner, move forward again to make distinctions and revisions.

That edge of either failure or success also occurs where teachers figure out what works best for a particular classroom, for a population's demographics, for each individual child. Students and teachers need to be encouraged to experiment without fear. Imagine trying to conduct a lab experiment in which the results are predetermined. What is learned? Inside, as well as outside, of laboratory settings we must continue to probe and measure, speculate and dissect, observe and revise. Experimentation is where we learn in every subject area.

What is wonderful about Dafoe's latest book on education policy is that it examines complications and concerns with the recent batch of reform initiatives under different administrations, yet Dafoe's rhetoric is simultaneously sane and humane, as well as probing and inventive. I have always believed that an educator who is creating in order to engage students is an educator who will become successful over time.

Like my STEM colleagues, Dafoe appreciates the critical role science and mathematics play in our country's future, but she also asks us to consider the equally significant role of humanities' courses. If STEM education is to be successful, the movement needs to do more than simply add a letter for all of the humanities. This is not an either/or equation. Nor should it be.

Approach is everything, Dafoe suggests, so we should stop and reflect, analyze and consider, continuously challenge, risk and create, encourage rather than demean, advance rather than settle. We want the best for our students and for our country. Let us begin with questions. I am on board.

Sally B. Mitchell,
2015–2016 Albert Einstein Distinguished Educator Fellow,
James Bryant Conant Award winner for teaching in chemistry, and
nationally recognized educator

NOTE

1. Valerie Strauss, "Key PISA Test Results for US Students," *Washington Post* (December 3, 2013), accessed November 20, 2015, https://www.washingtonpost.com/news/answer-sheet/wp/2013/12/03/key-pisa-test-results-for-u-s-students/.

Preface

Strangeness of Ideas

There is water on Mars! In all likelihood, it appears that water in liquid form is in evidence on the planet Mars.[1] Until recently, this statement would be met with laughter or derision. Every day, it seems, we are confronted with the startling and new until it becomes more widely accepted and then enculturated. What was once strange eventually appears conventional in science and, sometime later, in the larger social context. Science and technology are, indeed, amazing. Language that allows expression of all that we do, think, and feel is equally amazing. Art that communicates on multiple levels and to various senses simultaneously is no less incredible.

A quick scan of the October 19, 2015, edition of the *New York Times* revealed, "new technology makes it possible to search for art based on color—and from the privacy of one's personal computer or mobile device."[2] In that single statement is the coalescence of science, technology, art, and language working to better human life. These disciplines are interconnected in so many ways that we seldom stop to consider how they are working together, focused as we are on divisions and specialization.

As I wandered around an unfamiliar antique store, these were the thoughts I was toying with when my musing was disrupted by another find of a slightly less profound nature. Standing there on a dusty shelf—behind a Chinese vase and broken picture frame—in a sprawling antiques warehouse in the mountains of western Virginia was a hand-carved Don Quixote, missing his lance but otherwise perfectly intact. For the slight sum of $5.00, plus tax, I could take him home with me.

Deliberating on Miguel de Cervantes's delusional but noble hero, Don Quixote's impotence, his arm flailing helplessly as he attempts to fight injustice, real or imagined, I reflected on Cervantes's larger-than-life character when I started writing this book because the battles I decided to enter have already been won, according to policymakers on both sides of the political aisle. Nevertheless, I set out to fight the giants.

Unlike "the Knight of the Woeful Countenance," however, I am not deluded, seeing monsters where there are only windmills. I have some of the skepticism and exactness of a scientist in me, too. I entered this project doubtful about moving policymakers but still hopeful that reasonable people, the American public, will continue to consider and reconsider ideas, analyze our progress and mistakes, and examine how we fund education and the purposes of those behind reform financing. I am also optimistic that our nation will remain open to the idea of questioning while working to create better public education that best serves students in the United States.

In wrestling with concepts and apt metaphors for this book, I knew I needed to focus on funding in some manner because it is the money beneath the foundations of education that is, in many respects, driving reform policy rather than the inverse. I briefly considered "Second Class Citizens" as a title when I was feeling particularly pessimistic, the appellation indicating an inherent hierarchy in recent years of education reform, as well as the collateral damage of mandates and policy directives.

Participating in an American Federation of Teachers (AFT) teleconference, led by AFT president, Randi Weingarten, with around 165,000 people on the evening of December 17, 2015, I came to the conclusion that the new Every Student Succeeds Act (ESSA) federal legislation attempts to undo some of the damage of the No Child Left Behind and Race to the Top policies, but it is difficult to turn around years of legislative mandates that have already been implemented.

In addition, three of the four most impactful strands of policy directives remain in effect under ESSA. Only the Common Core is uncoupled from mandate status in ESSA,[3] not testing tied to teacher evaluations. In addition, individual states have already implemented the Common Core, so even that effort to untangle the problems of the Common Core is fraught with issues for years to come.

Alternative titles for this book became chapter headings here because the force of the underlying ideas necessitated a place in this discourse that asks for reopening discussions on education reform, raising questions rather than supporting dogma or complacently accepting less for students and our children.

In preparation for writing, I continued to come across the phrase, the "strangeness of ideas," as if this wording had entered the educational reform lexicon surreptitiously, but, of course, the phrase feels right because all new ideas are initially strange. We are the one species that has the awareness to scrutinize the oddity of ideas—analogies and metaphors, moving from one abstraction to another, whether played like musical notes in a mathematical equation, the poetry in a metaphysical discussion, or one in which writers, artists, and physicists consider origins, the biology of a novel, the body hiding the DNA strands in the symbols of language.

We can and should be a nation of readers and writers, scientists, musicians, mathematicians, artists, and historians. Presently, however, this notion of strengthening our interdisciplinary approaches equally or in harmonious tension may be one of the strangest as education reform policy is laid out before us.

What is the current direction(s) of American education reform? This charge could best be summed up through three strands that remain with us: STEM, expansion of charter schools/privatization of schools, and linking teacher job security to student achievement through test scores on measurements, originally developed in conjunction with the Common Core standards, and now through state-mandated curricula.

Although proponents of the STEM education movement will make a claim for the "newness" of STEM, it is already familiar to everyone who understands history or is old enough to have experienced the Cold War days when the United States and the former Soviet Union were dangerously engaged in an ideological battle that held nuclear weapons over our heads as the ultimate silencer of debate. Yet fear propelled everyone to the moon and back before the impetus petered out for a time. Historians can date the political agenda for STEM education to the post–World War I era.[4]

When we understand our history, we are able to intelligently return to ideas and reformulate, rethink, and recast in powerful ways that are not always helpful, but as long as we are willing and able to raise questions, returning to the past to reflect on what we have learned is anything but dangerous or wasteful. Questions about the current education reform movement, however, have too often been stifled, even silenced. The bipartisan effort on ESSA, however, does give pause and offer hope that both sides of the political aisle can work together to produce better results.

Education reform, as conceived over the last twenty years at least—largely designed by politicians and business owners who stand to make enormous profits from a profusion of tests, as well as setting up private schools—appears predetermined. But American optimism and curiosity are notoriously hard to kill. With this text, we venture into these waters, resolving to examine, using logic, history, creative writing, scientific inquiry, and the metaphor to persuade people to again ask questions about the expressway to STEM only and charter schools, about reforms designed as one size fits all across approximately 10,000 school districts in the nation.

As one colleague said recently, "STEM and charter schools are here to stay. Get used to it." We appear to be on yet another fast-track without questioning the implications, this one clearly favoring expansion of charter or private schools—often misleadingly calling this development parent choice—and expanding STEM education and STEM schools as the only model for improving students' sciences and mathematics academic performances.

Since the definitions of STEM education vary widely, but all focus on science, technology, engineering, and mathematics, it would seem that a good starting place would be a discussion about the importance of each of those fields. Yet this approach, too, can be deceptive. Is STEM education really about science or only about particular sciences that may be used in "building engineers?" Is the study of mathematics truly represented in the STEM model, or is applied math, as related to solving problems in engineering, intended? These are questions that have not been addressed by those who are dictating educational policies and models.

We want to remain open to alternatives and variations in creating real improvements in education and the lives of children. Education reform is too important to children, our society, and civilization to leave to wealthy businessmen who intend to cut up the multi-billion-dollar education market to further increase their fortunes.

Let us start here: before we can fix a problem, we have to first identify the underlying issues, and the underlying matters of contention are far more complicated than this current group of policymakers are admitting. Hiding or masking an issue will not cause it to go away but to fester. We must begin by questioning the policies and policymakers who have politicized possible solutions.

Questioning authority causes tensions partially because every new idea is strange before the notion takes hold. In *A Beautiful Question: Finding Nature's Deep Design*, Noble Prize winning scientist Frank Wilczek writes, "[B]y exploring how great thinkers struggled and often went astray, we gain perspective on the initial strangeness of ideas that have become, through familiarity, too 'obvious' and comfortable."[5]

Wilczek asks his readers to consider Galileo's (among many others) odd ideas. Imagine the powerful, adherent Catholics who first learned of Galileo's mathematical propositions involving Earth encircling the sun, placing man not at the center of the universe, not even at the center of the solar system, not at a center at all. This view was not only heretical at the time but frightening to nearly everyone around him, and Galileo was placed under house arrest, fortunate not to lose his life.

Returning to the ideas found in Nobel Prize winning author Wilczek's new book, we discover a perfect symbol of the necessity of interdisciplinary study. The cover of *A Beautiful Question: Finding Nature's Deep Design* is riveting: wrapped in a cream-colored jacket with a hole die-cut at the center, the title and author's name symmetrically balanced above and below.

At the center of the cover—peering out at the reader—is a small portion of the artwork of an early cosmology map, which is fully exposed in all its colorful, fantastic, and intricate design once the jacket is removed. Here is an esteemed scientist reaching the wider audience not through his science alone but through his writing skills, his understanding of human history, and the instant appeal of his cover art, as well as its design.

Thinking ourselves advanced, America does not declare people with peculiar ideas to be heretics and directly threaten their lives, but Americans, and every other people on Earth, still struggle when they are confronted with new theories; innovators are frequently regarded with deep suspicion, and may, in fact, be in trouble in some parts of their communities because of their groundbreaking hypotheses.

We are more likely to lose our career posts and financial security, rather than our lives, for our original ideas, but these are still losses. Losing a job may even mean homelessness. More likely, however, innovative ideas die without an audience because the control of the message is directly and indirectly related to power, politics, and big money. Influence rather than arrest stops us.

Wilczek is credited with "proving" the "existence of a remarkable new light particle, the axion,"[6] but the strangeness of the discovery of a new particle is not met with hostility or fear simply because this information is available to, and known by, a relatively small number of people (other scientists studying particle theories). The general public is not confronted with a problem at the introduction of the axion or color gluons because most people have no knowledge of such an existence; discussion is confined within a narrow band of this professional, and highly specialized, community.

How many people will read about the incredible findings of two American scientists (Aziz Sancar is also Turkish) and a Swedish scientist who just won the 2015 Nobel Prize in Chemistry for their work in DNA repair?[7] Although their work is immensely exciting and cutting-edge, the names of Americans Paul Modrich and Aziz Sancar, as well as Tomas Lindahl, are likely to remain unrecognized in the wider culture, at least in the United States. In some respects, this is a cultural rather than an educational failing.

In order to understand exactly what these scientists did to receive this recognition, however, we have to understand a lot of science—DNA, cell division, cells "correcting errors," UV damage to cells, mismatching nucleotides, enzymes, DNA polymerase, mapping at the molecular level—yet their incredible findings may lead to new treatments for cancer, among other profoundly important uses. We should know the names of these scientists and understand the work they do. Here is yet another powerful argument for improving our educational offering in science and mathematics in public schools.

When we are focused on STEM education only, however, there is also a potent counter-argument to be made that technology instruction is and has been integrated into every area of concentration in public schools for a number of years. How effective has that integration been? What has been less successful is creating time for teachers to work across disciplines to create meaningful and strategic interdisciplinary lessons and instruction. Although professional development is part of nearly every public school year plan, the actual hours that teachers have to spend on working together is largely nonexistent.

Why does it matter that a science and an art teacher get planning time together? One step in this disposition is suggested by Edward O. Wilson in his text *The Meaning of Human Existence*, as found in the epigraph to this text. Professor Emeritus Wilson of Harvard advances the idea that we need a much more interdisciplinary approach to excite students about science and mathematics, but we also need to consider the sources of concepts within our culture and identity, promoting the humanities as zealously as STEM subjects.

We need education reform that considers all of the variables that impact a child's education. Our children deserve an education that not only allows but encourages questioning, fosters intellectual growth, and, yes, transformation. Reform should not be top-down, based on the size of profits for venture capitalists or remain in the catchy sound bite domain of politicians looking to improve their poll numbers. Public education is too important as the foundation of our democracy to be damaged or destroyed by either complicity with business interests or indifference to changes that dismantle rather than build, politicize rather than problem solve.

NOTES

1. "Evidence for more recent clay formation on Mars discovered." *ScienceDaily*, Brown University (December 14, 2015), accessed December 15, 2015, www.sciencedaily.com/releases/2015/12/151214150129.htm.

2. Laura Van Straaten, "The New Digital Art Service That Puts Color First," *Art Matters, New York Times* (October 19, 2015), accessed November 10, 2015, http://www.nytimes.com/2015/10/19/t-magazine/art-matches-decor-service.html?_r=0.

3. Every Student Succeeds Act (ESSA), US Department of Education (December 2015), http://www.ed.gov/esea.

4. Improving Undergraduate STEM Education, "Synopsis of Program," National Science Foundation (November 11, 2006), accessed October 19, 2015, http://www/nsf.gov/pubs/2015/nsf15526/nsf15526.htm.

5. Frank Wilczek, *A Beautiful Question: Finding Nature's Deep Design* (New York: Penguin Press, 2015), 3.

6. Wilczek, *A Beautiful Question*, 337.

7. Jade Walker, "3 Win the 2015 Nobel Prize in Chemistry for Studies in DNA Repair," *Huffington Post*, AOL (October 7, 2015), accessed October 8, 2015, http://www.huffingtonpost.com/entry/nobel-prize-in-chemistry_5614c8d7e4b021e856d2d368.

Acknowledgments

My deepest gratitude is extended to Dr. Thomas Koerner, vice president and editorial director of Rowman & Littlefield, Inc., for his continued leaps of faith in me to create books that matter in education.

I would also like to thank the following people who read early drafts and encouraged me in this endeavor to bring about more meaningful, educational policy discussions: my family members, Colette, Nicole, Daniel, and Blaise Dafoe; my colleagues and friends in education, Karen Hempson, Cindy Hlywa, Pamela Herrington, Keith Ward, Amanda Ward, Lisa McDougal, Joy Kelleher, Barb Crossett, Dr. Mary Kennedy, Dr. Karla Alwes, Dr. Karen Pastorello, Susan Cerretani, and Jennifer Kirchoff; all of my new National League of American Pen Women (NLAPW) friends, Janet Fagel, Rachael Ikins, and Mary Gardner, in particular; fellow writers and poets Jo Pitkin and Gwynn O'Gara; and my many students who have been a continuous source of inspiration over the years.

In addition, I must single out a few former students who were voices behind the inspiration for this book: Jeff Owens, whose student work appears in the book, with his gracious permission; Cole Greabell, Colleen Adler, Danielle LaRose, and, most particularly, Katherine and Grace Babcock, who read early drafts and the abstract, commented on the content, and discussed ideas for the book with me.

I would like to thank the author of the foreword to this book, Sally B. Mitchell, who remains as passionate about chemistry and teaching as I am about English and education. We met seventeen years ago as we started our careers at the same high school in Central New York.

Lastly, I must extend thanks to the generous professional writers and educators who gave me permission to quote from their material, Brian Malone and Alan J. Singer, who read my book abstract. I am deeply grateful to Edward O. Wilson, who graciously allowed me to use a quotation from his work as my epigraph.

Introduction

Examples and Non-Examples

This book is about how education policy informs or misinforms, leads to positive change or causes additional problems for educators and students. It is also about the authentic values of education and the importance of formulating questions in order to learn. I wanted to create a text that was not just another data-driven paper or a series of well-researched statements of fact. Those texts have already been written (see appendix A). Another approach is needed if we are to reopen the reform discussions again or engage others in a dialogue, Socratic or otherwise, about education policy.

The essential question of this text is one that intersects the study of art and language, scientific inquiry and history: the "beautiful question" is an artistic and historical pursuit as much as a scientific/mathematical one. And it is a question that could not be fully explored without mastery in all of these disciplines.

From the outset, I made the decision to play with language and the vessels of discourse, encouraging readers to have some fun along the way, even though we are dealing with the very serious subject of educating our nation's young. We can enjoy the adventure of exploring policy ideas and the ways in which policy is created. For these reasons, I chose to incorporate narratives, a menu, chart, parody, and poetry, in addition to more traditional essay structures, to frame my rhetoric.

For some, the format presented here may, indeed, appear strange. The text morphs into various creative shapes intended to catch the eyes and ears of readers with sundry approaches to information. The text as a whole, however, offers a compelling argument about education policy. The design is intended to stimulate dialogue and allow further consideration of alternatives to the current path(s) of education reform.

Considering various teaching strategies as models, I would like to offer an easy to follow rationale for my intentions and design of this book. Using the instructional strategy of example and non-example in introducing *Misdirection of Education Policy*, I begin with non-examples:

- This book is not a research paper, master's thesis, or PhD dissertation, although it evolved out of years of action research and teaching practice in actual classrooms.

- It is not a plea for maintaining the status quo in public education.
- It is not a defense or attempt at defense of poor teaching or teachers.
- This work is not an indictment of well-meaning educators and administrators.
- It is not an exercise in or deliberate dive into edu-speak.
- It is not a shielding of unions or their responsibility in helping to promote reforms.
- It is not an indictment of unions or anti-union rallying cry.
- It is not a history of teaching in America or history of pedagogical practice. Those books have been written. See appendix A.
- It is neither a rant nor a venting of angry reaction to recent diatribes against teachers, unions, and public schools.
- It is not—by any means—anti-science or mathematics or engineering.
- It is not a defense of the humanities since they need no aegis.
- It is not a reaction to a poor review in the Annual Professional Performance Review (APPR) process.
- It is neither radical nor revolutionary in ideology.
- It is not a workshop topic, although educators might enjoy workshops developed around some of the concepts raised here that are apropos in their classrooms.
- It is not a single answer or definitive statement about a solution to the very complex socioeconomic, political, historical, and cultural problems that interfere with students' education and their academic performance, as well as teachers' ability to help them make intellectual progress.

By way of comparison and contrast, I offer what I intend in the writing and publication of this book:

- Raising questions about the direction(s) of education "reform"
- Causing discussions about whom should be actively involved in, as well as leading, education reforms
- Posing queries about the respective values of the humanities and STEM paths
- Encouraging discussions about funding sources and considering the reason these individuals and groups are behind purported education "reform"
- Inciting divergent thinking and passionate discourse about education that is centered on children and learning
- Questioning the exclusionary practices at the heart of aspects of the current education "reform" movement
- Examining possible ulterior motivations that lie behind the charter school and STEM impetus

- Inducing scholarly discourse about the current "reforms" and possible alternatives
- Provoking the searching mind
- Considering how to best develop and nurture the searching mind in students and educators
- Beginning conversations about how we frame rhetoric on this topic
- Precipitating the entrance of educators and students and their "strange" ideas into the reform conversation
- Empowering teachers, students, and the public in an area of education where they are too often left with the consequences of top-down mandates and policies
- Advancing knowledge about public education, charter schools, testing, STEM, and career-to-work education through discourse
- Compelling discussions about what takes place in actual classrooms, as opposed to some idealized (and unattainable) version
- Examining some of the consequences of current reform initiatives
- Advocating for a larger role for teachers, students, and parents in the "engineering" of education reform

It is important to note that intentions are outlined as phrases not statements, leaving ample room for conversation and discovery, as well as revision of ideas. A discourse about education should be open-ended and continue to remain open. We will be better architects of reform if we listen to more voices. This book is—in brief—about asking questions and the ideas relating to the wisdom and funding of American public education reform.

ONE
We're Funding the Left Side of Your Brain

Techno-scientific is the term being applied everywhere we look, signifying the marriage of technology and the social context of the applied sciences propelling our advances in mechanization. Technology is the smart, sexy, good-looking, athletic son with everything he is wearing talking to everything else he is wearing, including his 3-D glasses, his mobile phone and computer, even his 3-D printed gun. He is the one getting all of his parents' attention and the gifts of new handheld devices, a new sports car loaded with every gadget, a huge increase in his allowance.

While his siblings? Well, they are building resentment in the attic. If Technology were an only child, all of this might have worked out for a while. For a number of reasons, Americans have been treating Technology as the only child and spoiling him rotten. Fortunately for children and our civilization, a few of his siblings are also at work on the architecture of rhetoric in every subject, painting and making music, foreign language and history, conducting science that has little or no direct relationship to building another handheld device.

The inherent problem in this techno-scientific global culture is its lopsidedness. By now, we should know that both hemispheres of our brains are necessary and interdependent, but old myths about poorly understood brain dominance theory persist with the left side of the brain not only associated with but exclusively responsible for reasoning, numbers, and critical thinking. How ideas are generated by the two hemispheres in our brains "talking" to each other has not made its way into the larger culture. Unfortunately, layperson psychology myths are still with us, not only about how a complex brain actually functions but how integrally important all subjects are for learning, experiencing, and approaching life.

Even if we agree that many of the ideas we conceive arise in different parts of our brain, we need, like our brains need, that communication. We are better scientists if we are also great readers of literature and history, artists, and designers. We are better mathematicians if we are also capable of understanding symmetry in language and the arts. We are also better thinkers when we delve deeply into sciences other than those that directly support advances in technology. We should support an approach to education that allows this kind of creative, cross-curricula instruction and learning.

In 1990, Stephen R. Covey wrote in his well-known work *Principle-Centered Leadership*, "Research on brain theory helps us to understand why some people are excellent producers but poor managers or great managers but weak leaders."[1] Covey made distinctions and predictions about what kind of a leader someone will be based upon brain dominance theory: "The research basically indicates that . . . the left works more with logic, the right works more with emotions."[2]

If Covey's literature had never been applied to education and decisions about policies regarding education, perhaps these statements would seem relatively innocuous, but Covey's work, too, has played a role in professional development for teachers and for the policymakers governing public schools. Covey's statement, "[W]e might say that we live in a left brain dominant world"[3] is one of the pillars upon which the push for STEM education rests.

It is not a leap for education reform leaders to jump to mandates that STEM is necessary for a left brain dominant world, except for the fact that layperson understanding of the left brain/right brain theory has largely been discredited. Scientists very much need the right hemisphere of their brains in order to do science, and poets need their left hemispheres to create, develop, and perform.

In the summer 2015 issue of Colgate University's *Colgate Scene* magazine, interim president Jill Harsin wrote in her message, discussing the unusual occurrence of twelve professors simultaneously retiring and the inevitable changes, "Proponents of the liberal arts do not always explain themselves very effectively in the face of challenges from those who support only the teaching of skill sets currently needed by employers."[4] We are being asked to educate our young within the narrow context of filling job slots and industry needs.

If we determine that the only value of education is to place students into business and industry positions, we should immediately begin to wonder which employers do not need people who communicate effectively, persuasively, and powerfully? Which employers need employees who have no sense of context or history? It would also be interesting to consider the employers who want perspective employees to come to the table with no sense of identity, ethics, or appreciation of others, formed in the seeds of language and the arts.

Harsin's comment is part of that larger conversation but felt as criticism by many educators—even if not intended to be so—because teachers and professors are experiencing similar frustrations forced into defending the humanities courses to students, administrators, and the public. Why should educators have to defend disciplines that are at the heart of all human exchange and the building of civilization and bonds between us? Behind these "conversations" are politics and policies, as well as a straight shot to funding sources.

As state and federal funding is reduced and directed to STEM subjects and STEM initiatives or entire STEM schools—whatever that means—politicians and administrators have moved emphasis to some areas of education over others, automatically giving greater weight to very particular areas of the curriculum and fields of study, to some teachers, and to the interests and concerns of certain students over others. The Commission on STEM Education: National Science and Technology Council released a presidential report in May 2013, directing schools across the country to help "prepare 100,000 excellent STEM teachers over the next decade."[5]

Is a student who is interested in becoming an engineer to be treated differently and far better than one who is interested in becoming a musician or a writer, a foreign correspondent or a pediatrician? What the shift in emphasis will accomplish has not yet been determined, but there are other possible outcomes that are not positive in nature.

Examination of exactly what is intended by STEM education is difficult because there is little agreement on exactly what STEM is other than identifying the acronym. Depending on your audience, the definition of the acronym and what is intended for education reform shifts shapes. Is the education model intended to have students explore all scientific fields or only those related to engineering? Does the acronym intend for students to explore culture and identity, and if so, how is the STEM model implemented?

It is telling the definitions have come from outside, leaving educators to try to make room for various other subjects and students whose passions run to something other than engineering. This practice is demoralizing for both students and faculty.

Perhaps a more direct approach is needed in order to engage policymakers on this issue. We could simply ask the people behind those funding sources, "which side of the human brain do you wish to support?" Yes, there are jobs in engineering in the year 2015. Yet some of our largest engineering firms have already turned away qualified American applicants in favor of hiring cheaper, young engineers abroad.

Of course, technology has changed the way the world operates—not necessarily for the better, but that is another essay—but do we need to communicate as engineers? Do we need to look at multiple perspectives from various positions in order to come to more innovative ways of problem solving? The answer to those questions is too obvious, so let us propose even more elementary questions:

- Is job training or "career readiness" the only goal of education?
- Are there outside factors that alter the course of a student's academic and career trajectory?
- Are there outside factors that continually shift emphasis in the global market?
- Are there diverse circumstances that negatively influence a student's ability to learn?
- Should students be tracked at younger ages into specific engineering and technology slots?
- Will students likely change their minds and hearts about what they want to do with their lives once they leave formal schooling?
- Are the proposed reforms really designed to help children become better students?
- Are the students' interests at work in the latest public education reform movement, a movement that has little or nothing to do with children?

If we simply examine possible answers to those questions, we will arrive at an obvious conclusion: our current reform movement is largely misdirected. We need the humanities as deeply and clearly as we need technology or applied sciences and mathematics and all that they "produce."

How is this political leaning toward the expansion and unequal funding of only certain sciences and applied mathematics determined by policies and legislation? Anyone with even a passing familiarity of the transformation taking place in public schools and colleges knows there are both unwritten and written mandates to create STEM curricula and STEM schools. Students are directly being told to pursue engineering careers at younger and younger ages.

Although the definition of STEM education has been imprecisely defined by administrators, politicians, business people, and government entities, the acronym alone suggests more than simply a narrow focus; this is an education principally based upon Applied Science, Technology, Engineering, and Applied Mathematics. Many of the sciences and areas of mathematics are also given short shrift, to say nothing of language, foreign languages, the arts, history, sociology, and psychology.

Should we be promoting mathematics and sciences in schools? The answer is obvious, but we should also be asking why engineering, technology, mathematics, and sciences are important only through their relationship to expanding technology and filling the requirements for engineering career readiness. If we only look to advance certain sciences and engineering in schools, we will likely find ourselves in one of those imagined-turned-very-real-dystopian stories.

Scientists and engineers are not the only ones to ask, "how do we do it?" Humanities also cause us to ask, "Why are we doing this? What does this mean in terms of who we are and the value of this endeavor?" Ethical and philosophical considerations are perhaps even more important today than the new technological territory being explored. Not everything we can do is something we should do. It is not our manifest destiny to go as far as we possibly can technologically, without ever questioning the wisdom or ethics of these "advancements."

Very soon, we will be facing a world in which technology has made it possible for business to operate without human beings, for every human defect to be engineered out of existence, for an entirely designed human. What does any of this mean? What role should education play in posing questions?

An example of this imbalance may be found in New York State, which recently began granting large stipends for master teachers who meet particular qualifications. Only math and science teachers are allowed to apply. Does this funding encourage better teaching in mathematics and science courses? That question has yet to be answered or even examined, but it certainly has the opposite effect on teachers of, and students interested in, the humanities.

Why should we value only half of the brain? Why aren't all teachers encouraged and/or rewarded for successful teaching practices? Why aren't all fields of instruction valued and children encouraged to pursue their interests and passions in diverse fields of study? Why should guidance counselors be encouraging every child to become an engineer?

Even if we take the lowest common denominator and decide to rebuild education solely on a foundation of job and career readiness, who knows exactly what today's children will be facing when they leave formal schooling? We certainly did not make accurate predictions about the world we live in eighteen years ago, or eighteen years before that, or eighteen years before that. In other words, this approach is short-sighted and will have unintended and, perhaps, disastrous results.

The rapidity of technological change will likely make human engineers, as well as millions of other careers, irrelevant in the not-too-distant future. Emphasizing only technology will likely make us all obsolete, as artificial intelligence will become increasingly dominant.

The role of the humanities has been taken for granted for so long that too many people are simply unable to articulate its paramount importance well, but, as for the role of writing, that question is central. One of the best responses comes from the British novelist Graham Greene: "Writing is a form of therapy; sometimes I wonder how all those who do not write, compose, or paint can manage to escape the madness, melancholia, the panic and fear which is inherent in a human situation."[6]

We can, and must, do better. Education should promote the formulating of original questions, critical thinking and reasoning, an interdisciplinary approach across fields of study, valuing each area of scholarship, building upon areas of concentration with other areas of study for each child. How are we to communicate in a global market without understanding other people, foreign languages? Painting is not possible without chemistry of pigments. But chemistry also needs that artist who asks for these paints.

America should value the whole child and each child. We must recognize that our current education reform is, unintentionally, creating another type of serious lack. While we are expanding our technology unfettered, the emotional, intellectual, aesthetic, and ethical growth of our children is being stunted.

NOTES

1. Stephen R. Covey, *Principle-Centered Leadership*, New York: Simon & Schuster (1990), 247.
2. Covey, *Principle-Centered Leadership*, 247.
3. Ibid., 247.
4. Jill Harsin, *Colgate Scene*, Colgate University (Summer 2015).
5. Executive Office of the President of the United States, National Science and Technology Council Report, May 2013, accessed 11 January 2015, https://www.whitehouse.gov/sites/default/files/microsites/ostp/stem_stratplan_2013.pdf.
6. Graham Greene, *Ways of Escape*, from "Books of the Times," Christopher Lehmann-Haupt, Review (January 8, 1981), accessed November 7, 2015, https://www.nytimes.com/books/00/02/20/specials/greene-escape2.html.

TWO
"If I Didn't Write in This Journal..."

"A writer's material is what he cares about," stated American writer John Gardner in an interview he gave in 1979.[1] Gardner went on to say in the *Paris Review*, "The novelist pursues questions and pursues them thoroughly."[2]

Pursuing questions is not only the work of a novelist but should be the work of education and educators, in general. It is the work of the history teacher and student, students and teachers of mathematics and the sciences. Pursuing questions also lies beneath the passion of artists in every medium. Let us start with our most basic charge as educators and citizens: We must help our children survive first and then thrive.

In a recent lecture through the Rosamond Gifford Lecture Series, the Irish/American writer Colum McCann stated, "reading literature, telling our stories and listening to stories" is necessary for "engaging otherness," allowing us to learn to empathize with other people and to work toward peace.[3] These are no mean goals. Yet where do we find these vitally important aspects of teaching our children in the current STEM conversation? Where do we find conversations about peace in a world bent on waging war and implementing new technologies with which to wage war?

Considering the terms being used by politicians, policymakers, and administrators in setting the agendas for STEM education, we will not likely come across the students' needs that are most critical for daily survival. Of course, they need employment, but they also need to be able to wake up and cope the next day and the day after that. They need to learn to consider other perspectives, diverse people, and various viewpoints. Educating a child has to be about more than college and career readiness. The evidence of this is painfully apparent in actual classrooms and in our complicated, interconnected world in constant conflict.

Collecting her students' journals one Friday afternoon, a teacher, who had been interviewed, stated that she sat down to do a quick read after school hours were over. She stopped when she opened a blue spiral notebook decorated with photos of the student, some images altered with imaginative lines. Inside she met these words: "If I didn't write in this journal, I might have to kill someone every day of my life."

She said her first thought was, "do I have to report this?" Then she stated that she read the next line in her journal which read, "Don't worry, I'm not really going to hurt anyone or myself. I just get really frustrated and angry and sad, and this journal helps me keep going. I can deal."

What is it about writing—as opposed to a mathematics or science or technology class—that helps a child just "keep going?" Writing, language, and art are associated with identity, which is one of the reasons why many students take a poor grade on an English paper or an art assignment much harder than they do a poor grade in another course. Being able to express herself on a daily basis was much more, for this student, than getting a grade in a class or meeting graduation requirements. Writing was, for her, about survival.

Pulitzer Prize winning author Alice Walker once wrote, "Writing saved me from the sin and inconvenience of violence."[4] Walker's words return us to and reinforce those ideas found in our student's journal. Writing can save lives. It is that simple and that complex. When we examine the many purposes of education today, we seldom hear discourse on the importance of preserving life and identity, yet there is nothing more central to our existence. Writing and communication skills empower children and young adults, pull them out or keep them from sinking in quicksand.

While policymakers look to business leaders to provide guidance for education reform, based upon current job vacancies, the real "movers and shakers" are in the classroom waiting for an opportunity to be heard. Turning to a student to help define how and why writing is so central to survival in the world seems like a natural choice. Jeff Owens II was a senior in high school at the time he wrote this excerpt from his essay as an analysis of an Annie Dillard text. Although he may not have initially intended to create an argument for the essential role of the humanities, his text does so:

> Few endeavors allow for the complete expression of the human psyche in the same fashion as writing. It is remarkable that the arrangement of language, which is used every day to facilitate even the most simple of tasks, can evoke sentiments and realizations that would lie dormant otherwise. The process of learning to write closely parallels the development of consciousness that occurs naturally over the course of one's life. In writing, just as in life, young people tend to experience a crucial transition period as they become young adults.

> In her essay, "Write 'Til You Drop," Annie Dillard performs the task of advising young writers how to write effectively and with meaning. Through the course of her text, Dillard presents the central idea that passion and involvement are essential components to becoming a skilled writer.
>
> The initial and most prominent statement that Dillard presents in her essay is that writing is an endeavor of love. According to Dillard, an author writes what he "alone loves at all" (1), which she elaborates by introducing multiple allusions and metaphors involving other authors. . . . This enthrallment with the world that surrounds us is a defining aspect of humanity, and writing is the tool utilized to chronicle the discoveries that occur not only in the outside world but within ourselves.
>
> Writing is both the summation and dissection of our life experience. It is how we record our history and share ideas, but most importantly, it is the scuba tank that provides the oxygen of epiphany while diving deep into an ocean of uncertainty. Dillard expresses the idea only passion can unlock potential as both young scholars and writers.[5]

This young man is studying chemistry in college, but his work as a writer and humanities scholar will enlarge his understanding of science and all other subjects. His ability to express his ideas metaphorically yet clearly will serve him well in any endeavor he undertakes.

We will never successfully educate our young citizens until we begin to recognize that writing and identity are intrinsically linked, that the discovery of their passions is central to their scholarship, and that the skills learned and experiences encountered in English courses, foreign language, history, and the arts are transferable to nearly every undertaking in life. Telling our life stories is central to our discoveries, key to avoiding psychosis, and crucial to our interactions with others in the world.

In a recent lecture in Syracuse, New York, Shakespeare scholar Stephen Greenblatt stated, "We have a compulsion not only to leave something behind but to tell a story," in his literary, historical, social, and scientific remarks made in the lecture "Age Is Unnecessary," a line from *King Lear*.[6] It is part of our makeup, suggested Greenblatt, this search through our literature and history, "speaks to some larger truth."[7] Greenblatt also advanced the idea of interwoven subject matters in education when he said, "There is no break between what history is and what science is."[8] In this seemingly straightforward and relatively simple statement is a radical idea for education reform.

Education reform should always involve teachers, administrators, and students across all disciplines in discussions. It must also involve communities. In Rob Reich's article "To Hell with Good Intentions: School Reform Is Failing America's Children," appearing in the November 2015 *Boston Review*, Reich comments on Dale Russakoff's book and the infusion of money into one New Jersey school district, noting outsiders' "hubris in seeing Newark as a 'proof point' for nation reform."[9]

Reich quotes Russakoff's words of contention, in her conclusion to *The Prize: Who's in Charge of America's Schools*, that reformers damned their best efforts before beginning: "'The reformers never really tried to have a conversation with the people of Newark.' This, she thinks, doomed the effort."[10] Top-down and drop-down "reform" imposed on schools, teachers, and children by politicians, business professionals, and the occasional philanthropist will not last simply because these outside groups or individuals do not understand the people, the particular issues that doom seemingly "smart" solutions.

Likewise, professional development should be designed by teachers to help teachers come up with better strategies for guiding young people to make discoveries, not pigeonhole them into slots "needed" by any one specific industry. Professional development programs that are layered one upon another—in the attempt to cover as many bases as possible—too frequently end up being nothing more or less than confusing to the teaching faculty (see chapter 8: Public Education Paradigm Shifts Menu).

While the current education reform initiatives move into gymnasiums where STEM exhibition tables are set up to promote careers in technology and engineering, and business leaders are talking with perspective future employees, we should not be surprised to learn that too many of our children are seen leaving the buildings unnoticed. We cannot afford this disconnect as a society, as a culture, as a democracy, and as human beings who live not in isolation but as part of a complex, interdependent, dynamic world in which everything is continually in motion.

NOTES

1. John Gardner, *The Paris Review Interviews*, Vol. II (New York: Picador, 2007), 146.
2. Gardner, *The Paris Review Interviews*, 153.
3. Colum McCann, Rosamond Gifford Lecture Series, FOCL, Syracuse, New York (presented lecture on September 15, 2015).
4. Alice Walker, "Anything We Love Can Be Saved," accessed October 19, 2015, http://thinkexist.com/quotation/writing_saved_me_from_the_sin_and_inconvenience/262526.html.
5. Jeff Owens II, class essay for Nancy Dafoe's College Prep English, (March 2015).
6. Stephen Greenblatt, "Age Is Unnecessary," FOCL (lecture presented at Rosamond Gifford Lecture Series, Syracuse, New York, October 14, 2015).
7. Greenblatt, "Age Is Unnecessary."
8. Ibid.
9. Rob Reich, "To Hell with Good Intentions: School Reform Is Failing America's Children," *Boston Review* (November 2, 2015), accessed November 3, 2015, http://bostonreview.net/books-ideas/rob-reich-dale-russakoff-prize.
10. Rob Reich, "To Hell with Good Intentions," 1.

THREE

Why Aren't Schools Run Like Businesses?

Between policymakers from the business and political spheres, there are voices that have taken center stage, declaring American public education, "in crisis," "bankrupt," "an utter failure," "disastrous," and all kinds of negative, hyperbolic terms. Disconnect between these people who condemn public education and an actual classroom of human beings is profound. As president of the American Federation of Teachers, Randy Weingarten recently said of this reformer crew, "[they] wouldn't last 10 minutes in an actual classroom."[1]

In any classroom, they would also find young people of tremendous positive energy who are succeeding. But, like the rest of humanity, children come from all types of backgrounds and abilities, circumstances and situations. Whether they will be able to access the material, bring resources to their product, and express themselves effectively depends upon a wide variety of factors outside of classrooms.

"The reform movement nationwide increasingly saw closure and the creation of new institutions—as opposed to funding and reorganizing existing schools—as the way forward,"[2] wrote Jalani Cobb in a recent article in the August 31, 2015, issue of the *New Yorker*. The paradox of closing schools as a way to "move forward" is not lost on Cobb or his astute readers.

Closure of one business and then relocation or opening of new businesses overseas is a practice that became highly favorable in the United States in the early 1980s when the economies of India and China, among other countries, expanded dramatically. American businesses were able to take advantage of lower costs of doing business by paying lower wages than they could get away with in the United States. In fact, they were also able to get around numerous, costly legislation that protected

US children in the form of child labor laws by locating their factories in parts of the world where children are exploited routinely.

Cobb continues this line of questioning in his article, "What's Really at Stake when a School Closes?" with historical and sociological notes on Rahm Emmanuel's closing of schools in Chicago and Michelle Rhee's action of shutting the doors of two dozen schools in Washington, DC.[3] In these instances, Cobb suggests, decisions about public schools were made to mirror business practices, but he also warns, "Is the conversation about school closure really a proxy for something more subtle, complex, and intractable?"[4]

Quoting teacher James Eterno in his article, Cobb offers the teacher's words as possible explanation for that "intractable" problem:

> "We still had plenty of smart kids, but we had many more higher-needs kids, English-language learners. . . . Concentrations of high-needs students place a strain on schools, and," Eterno said, "We didn't get the support. We were not prepared to deal with the changing population." The tacit belief that large schools were unreformable meant that Jamaica's sliding numbers looked to some experts like predictable educational failure; to the faculty, those numbers looked like what happens when a school is asked to educate a challenging population without the necessary tools.[5]

Cobb identifies many of those factors that necessitated a change in how Jamaica High School teachers practiced their art and craft, but those circumstances also begged for a government response. The idea of closing schools suggests that policymakers giving up on solving some of the complex problems that beset our nation is unavoidable. We can start again somewhere else, but those same cultural, economic, and social issues that are plaguing contemporary public schools remain.

Businesses can cut and reorganize, shut down and locate overseas, lay off employees and hire cheap labor by reopening plants in Mexico, Bangladesh, China, and Southeast Asian countries. Businesses by their very nature are not run on a moral or ethical basis. They operate to make money and more money.

If a factory burns to the ground, taking at least 112 employees with it on the outskirts of Dhaka, Bangladesh, in just one of many of these horrific factory fires in the region,[6] the "losses" are numerically figured into the risk-management equation in economic terms. This is clear in that dangerous practices in these factories have continued in the face of these tragedies.

Human rights activists have campaigned for better business practices overseas, naming American companies that work with factories that are known "death traps," according to Ineke Zeldenrust, the international coordinator for the Clean Clothes Campaign. Zeldenrust recently remarked that American companies are responsible even if they do not own the factory with which they are working: "Their failure to take action amounts to criminal negligence."[7]

In a recent issue of the online journal, *E-Commerce Times* founder and managing partner at Capital Source Partners, Theodore F. di Stefano, wrote: "Outsourcing will continue. Think about this fact: The cost per month of health insurance for a US worker in many cases exceeds the total monthly wages of a Chinese worker. It's obvious why companies are so anxious to outsource their products or services to other countries."[8] The only consideration it would appear here in the business world is the size of the profit.

Business operates by its own set of rules, and the well-being of children, the health of a society, and the number of jobs lost or outsourced are simply not part of their equations. It is not coincidental that one of the ubiquitous terms in education for the past several years is the word "stakeholders."

If you teach or have ever taught in a public school setting, you have heard this question over and over: "Why aren't schools run more like businesses?" Why are we not "outsourcing" our students? Why are we not "outsourcing" special education students who are more costly to educate? Those are questions that every educator finds disturbing, yet those are questions that would be raised in business.

Setting up charter schools may not be intended to leave special needs children behind, but that will be one likely result. Privatizing schools is another way for certain communities to avoid the responsibilities of education of all of its children, particularly those who need very expensive special services.

Charter schools are largely free from many of the mandates for which public schools are held responsible, but public taxes still pay for many charter schools. Charter schools are, quite simply, a new big business, and business interests are everywhere in education today. Leaving many students behind by design and policy is simply unacceptable for America.

The *New York Times* recently ran an article about Intel ending its sponsorship of the Science Talent Search contest after funding it for seventeen years.[9] Examining the reasons the corporation gave for ending its backing, it was implied that they were simply cutting costs and that they had launched a new competition for international students:

> Gail Dundas, a spokeswoman for Intel, could not say why it was ending its support, but she said the company, which has struggled with a shift to mobile computing devices but is still one of the tech industry's most influential names, is "proud of its legacy" in supporting the award. . . . "Intel will continue to support a separate talent search aimed at international student competition at least through 2019, which is Intel's contractual term," said Ms. Dundas.[10]

Herein is a perfect example of a science and technology industry giant that is making business decisions at the same time it offers evidence of why schools should not be run more like a business. They made a business arrangement based on economics: to stop supporting science and technology education development in the United States through one of the most successful national science contests.

They came to an agreement to look for their budding engineers in other parts of the world, in a country or countries where the young engineers coming to them some day as perspective employees would be willing to work for lower wages, again, a monetary decision that would appear to undermine so much of what the current STEM school movement was created to appease, as well as the rationale for its emergence.

Do we really want our schools to be run like Intel? Business models are developed to produce something and control the "bottom line" for the greatest profitability. Programs are abandoned regardless of human loss or benefit because business finds more economical ways of getting their labor supply.

Businesses do not make agreements in order to find ways to hire more Americans. That is simply not the nature of the beast. Bottom line. Scrap may be stored until it can be sold in industry/business. Imperfect parts are excised. Factories are established in parts of the world where labor is cheap and workers' rights are few.

This is not a model that works particularly well with children. There is no bottom line when the "product" is a human being. Closing schools and outsourcing them to China, Vietnam, Indonesia, the Philippines, Pakistan, and India are not very helpful ideas when it comes to educating our youth.

Closing schools and firing all of the teachers, then reopening them under a charter model some (likely a long) time later, are not only tremendously disruptive practices to children's education, these practices offer no guarantee that the new charter school will help children academically achieve at a higher level than in the public school setting. Yet this was part of a national education policy until recently.

Undoubtedly, new teachers, who have been hired to take the place of all those fired because their students' test scores were low, will take time to acclimate to their roles and acquire the kind of deep knowledge within a discipline and wide assortment of strategy tools that excised teachers held. It is also likely that these new teachers came out of the same teacher preparation schools that helped produce the kinds of teaching practices that have been criticized.

What is seldom discussed in all of the political noise out there about charter schools is the fact that only in public schools are all children given an opportunity to be educated. No child is turned away from public schools because their parents can't afford the school, or because the child is not intellectually or physically gifted, or because the child has special needs, or because the child has struggled with behavioral problems, or because the child is a certain race, color, or religion. The last qualifier is particularly relevant in light of candidates' sound bites about our Muslim children.

Public schools accept all children: repeat, all children. Children without the ability to speak, without hearing, and who are struggling with mental illness or developmental disorders, including schizophrenia, autism spectrum disorders, bipolar disorders, anxiety disorders, depression, eating disorders, alcohol/substance abuse dependence, obsessive-compulsive disorder, severe physical deformities, attention-deficit/hyperactivity disorder (ADHD), disorder of written expression, expressive language disorder, separation anxiety disorder, social anxiety phobia, dissociative disorders, brain damage from birth or accidents, behavioral problems, Tourette's syndrome, stuttering, transient tic disorder, antisocial personality disorders, neurodevelopmental disorders, are all welcomed into public school classrooms.

In other words, all children in this country have a right to a free, public education. This is one of the hallmarks of our greatness as a country.

The charter school "reform" movement—whether it was created simply to make money or truly to help certain populations of students—has pulled a tremendous amount of tax money away from public schools that do all of the heavy lifting and diverted those tax dollars to particular sets within the larger population. At a time when public schools are dealing with more and more societal problems manifested in the schools, we are expected to meet all of the responsibilities and new mandates upon mandates with the same or less money.

We should be asking, "Which children should we educate? Which 'defective part' would you like us to get rid of? If we do a 'tolerance analysis' and decide certain 'parts' are simply too costly, should we determine not to accept the part at all? If some of the 'parts' are causing delay in the work flow, should we remove those parts from the assembly?"

Here is the issue broken down to its simplest terms: Children are not parts or scraps. They are not defective, and public schools will not "get rid of them" because some children do not meet certain standards upon entrance, although private charter schools are allowed to and do take these types of actions. Creating charter schools is not about creating "competition" for public schools but about funneling public money into private, corporate hands.

Public education should not be privatized or owned and operated by a corporation or corporations. In examining New York governor Andrew Cuomo's plan to privatize more schools, *New York Times* writer Kate Taylor noted, "Some schools receive support from financial-sector philanthropists who also were major contributors to the governor's re-election campaign" in her January 20, 2015, article "Cuomo's Education Agenda Sets Battle Lines with Teachers' Unions."[11] It should matter that we are aware of the funding behind social agendas because motive becomes means.

With campaign financing increasingly hidden on both sides of the political aisle, it becomes far too easy for business interests to dictate policy behind a figure-head of a political leader who is far too beholden to those interests. This concern also looms large as the shift from federal to more state control gradually takes place under the Every Student Succeeds Act (ESSA), and political winds and degrees of corruption vary from state to state, year to year.

A profusion of texts dedicated to forcing the equation of treating schools as businesses seems to conclude that we would be better off if we simply disbanded all public schools and made sure that we universally adopted business practices throughout the education system. It would certainly be more profitable for some.

Myron Lieberman wrote about the crisis and the failure of public schools for over thirty years. Lieberman's *The Teacher Unions: How They Sabotage Educational Reform and Why* purported to have the answer to educational reform: get rid of teachers' unions. His diction betrays anti-union bias at every turn: "unions stifle dissent, sabotage meaningful reform, and hold parents hostage to bureaucracy."[12] It sounds simple enough if it were accurate or not grossly oversimplified.

Lieberman also wrote policy texts for the politically conservative think tank, the Cato Institute, focusing on business models for schools, even using "Market Solutions to the Education Crisis" as the title of one text.[13] The business model for education has had a lasting appeal in this country even though the model's lack of effectiveness appears to demonstrate opposite results.

Are "market solutions" really the model we want for America's children? Examination of the market as model, on any given day, should give us pause if not cause us to shudder. Market fluctuations dependent on China's economy are not good models for education.

Peter Brimelow's *The Worm in the Apple: How the Teacher Unions Are Destroying American Education* is a text with a title that appears actually oddly humorous in its hyperbole, if it were not also deceptive and outrageous. American business has been engaged in an ideological and sometimes literal fight with unions since they began their fight to protect the basic rights and lives of workers. Brimelow's text is one in a barrage of like-minded works that appear to be about blame rather than solutions.

The temptation for big-moneyed interests to dictate not only policy but curriculum—what children should or should not read and consider—is too great, and ample evidence of this type of practice already exists. Business or political interests may decide that Thomas Jefferson needs to be excised from our history or that the slave trade was really a "worker" trade—replacing one word radically changes meaning.

Once the message is controlled, we lose the most basic concept of education. This is not paranoia but an examination of a clear progression. Who will ask the questions? How will "history" be framed and by whom? Who is left to attempt an analysis when the answers are already dictated?

At one point, our news media had thousands of outlets, and the messages were varied. Americans heard multiple voices. Today, we hear fewer messages. Our media is largely owned by far fewer corporations. What we hear is, to an increasing degree, controlled. If this trend continues, there will be fewer, if any, questions, only compliance. We lose the advantage of multiple perspectives and fall into line in a very dangerous fashion. In no time, we might not recognize our democracy or ourselves.

NOTES

1. Randy Weingarten, (2015), accessed December 17, 2015, http://www.aft.org/about/leadership/randi-weingarten.
2. Jalani Cobb, "What's Really at Stake when a School Closes?" Annuals of Education, *New Yorker*, Conde Nast (January 1, 2014), accessed August 31, 2015, http://www.newyorker.com/magazine/2015/08/31/class-notes-annals-of-education-jelani-cobb.
3. Cobb, "What's Really at Stake when a School Closes?"
4. Ibid.
5. Ibid.
6. Ali Manik and Jim Yardley.
7. Vikas Baja, "Fatal Fire in Bangladesh Highlights the Dangers Facing Garment Workers," *New York Times* (February 25, 2012), accessed September 10, 2015, http://www.nytimes.com/2012/11/26/world/asia/bangladesh-fire-kills-more-than-100-and-injures-many.html?_r=0.
8. Theodore F. di Stefano, "Why Money Chases Cheap Labor," *E-Commerce Times* (February 3, 2006), accessed September 30, 2015, http://www.ecommercetimes.com/story/48622.html.
9. Quentin Hardy, "Intel to End Sponsorship of Science Talent Search," Business Day, *New York Times* (September 9, 2015).
10. Ibid.
11. Kate Taylor, "Cuomo's Education Agenda Sets Battle Lines with Teachers' Unions," *New York Times*, (January 20, 2015), accessed October 12, 2015, http://www.nytimes.com/2015/01/21/nyregion/cuomos-education-agenda-sets-battle-lines-with-teachers-unions.html.
12. Myron Lieberman, "Market Solutions to the Education Crisis," *Policy Analysis* No. 75, Cato Institute (July 1,1986), accessed October 15, 2015, http://www.cato.org/pubs/pas/pa075.html.
13. Lieberman, "Market Solutions," 1.

FOUR
Faulty Logic, Public Discourse

Long after congressional and presidential candidates have been elected, defeated, moved to the background or foreground, their policy platforms frequently remain with us as part of a cultural dialectic. Like the boy who cried wolf, political candidates repeated pronouncements leave us with an aftermath or, in the very least, an aftertaste. The loaded words they use to get attention or notice are often left with us like a virus without cure.

Once public education has been repeatedly declared to be "in crisis" and "failing," the wider perception lingers almost independent of actual steps taken to reform and revise our educational offering. For this reason, examining the public statements made in policy discussions is important long after those candidates are either no longer relevant or dominating the political landscape. Their platforms and policy statements must continue to be analyzed and examined, not accepted as fact without verification.

New Yorker staff writer John Cassidy wrote in the October 2015 edition on a Noble Prize winning economist, titled "John Angus Deaton: A Skeptical Optimist Wins the Economics Nobel." In his article, Cassidy examines Deaton's thinking about economics and the controversy his ideas have generated. According to Cassidy, Deaton suggests, "the world is a complicated place and that reducing it to simple theories is almost always dangerous."[1]

Deaton's wise counsel would seem to be obvious, but over and over again, we have evidence of policy being made that truncates discussion about the complexity of theories and situations in the name of expediency or saving or making money. We see this evidence played out repeatedly in our electoral processes. Politicians are known for simplifying complex issues to create sound bites that are often misleading by intent.

Scholarly examination of the issues underlying students' academic performance failures would suggest that we need to confront a variety of social ills in order to get at the real problems in education, but policymakers have too often discounted the obvious for the "fixes" of privatizing education and creating STEM schools, or firing all the teachers. Abandoning knowledgeable conversation for sound bites, politicians from both major political parties in the United States have taken to repeating these notes, often without grounding their statements in logic or explicit evidence.

Signs at the end of 2015 indicated that the most powerful Democrat in the country at the time was changing policy position—Obama's call to educators to spend less time on test preparation appeared to be backing away from an earlier cry for teacher accountability—but his plea remains problematic.

If teacher "accountability" is still tied to student test scores and teachers are to spend less time on test preparation, how is this recipe fair or accurate? In addition, test measurements will now vary widely from state-to-state. In order to examine some of the problems inherent in these statements from our politicians, we need to know a little about logic, how it works, and what rhetorical tricks are employed.

Because rhetoric is used to persuade the public, it behooves the public to be aware of the ways in which information is manipulated and presented. According to accepted knowledge and study, Aristotle identified three types of logic used in persuasion:

- ethos (ethical wisdom often from authority figure)
- pathos (emotion)
- and logos (reason)

Rhetorical deception may be used to convince someone of a position based on false appeals other than logic or fact. The test shown on succeeding pages offers a glimpse at the kind of cultural dialectic we are left with after fiercely contested elections. Elections and officials come and go, but the rhetoric, the language remains with us.

Charter schools, value-added measurements (VAMs), massive open online courses (MOOCs), and teacher accountability are part of our conversations in education now and will be for a long time to come. It would appear that everyone had something to say about education reform, but the quotations in our "test" demonstrate a lack of logical arguments, deliberate deception, or lack of clear knowledge of the problems.

The wording in the test examples represents some of the thinking from a number of candidates on both sides of the political aisle for the highest office in our land. Many of these public figures may not be particularly relevant in policymaking in the future, but their wording—striking similar—will continue to be significant in the way discussions about education policy and reform are framed. Phrases such as "public schools are dangerous monopolies" become accepted by the public as fact rather than politically loaded diction.

Without further analysis, the culture shifts into accepting as the starting point of a dialectic: all public schools are paralyzed failures; no public schools have good graduation rates; charter schools are the answer; teachers are lazy and richly protected; unions are evil and must be done away with; schools are places where profits should be made; students should fill businesses' desired slots.

Far more important than the individuals referenced here is the fact that the wording represents ideology and platforms that are likely to be with us far longer than any of these public figures from both sides of the political aisle. If those platforms or positions are not grounded in fact or logic, we are left with an unfortunate legacy that continues to serve as a framework for discussion about education reform. Words do matter.

Ready for your formative assessment?

Directions: Mark the correct answer by completely filling in the circle. Be careful not to mark outside the lines.	(Cover this side before taking the test) **Answer Key**
1. Which of the following are actual statements about educators and public education made by public officials or people running for office? o A. "[I intend] to break what is in essence one of the only remaining public monopolies—and that's what this [public school] is, it's a public monopoly." o B. "And there are probably 10,000 extraordinary teachers. Let's find those teachers, put them on the internet and have them teaching most of our kids." o C. "If I were not president, but if I were king in America, I would abolish all teachers [sic] lounges, where they sit together and worry about, oh woe is us." o D. All of the above.	If you filled in circle D, you are correct. A. Statement by New York Governor Andrew Cuomo. Source: http://danielskatz.net/2014/10/31/andrew-cuomo-makes-it-official-hes-at-war-with-teachers/ B. Statement by Rand Paul. Source: Sullivan, 2. C. Statement made by Ohio Governor John Kasich. Source: http://www.huffingtonpost.com/entry/john-kasich-teachers-lounges_55d4bb94e4b055a6dab26670

Table 4.1, part one

| 2. Which of the following sentences were actually stated by public figures?

o A. "The Common Core is about a common sense set of standards that will help our students be prepared for college careers in life."
o B. "School choice gives low-income children the same choices and opportunities that children from wealthy families have always had. And school choice improves the public schools, making them stronger and more effective."
o C. "The first step is to recognize that expecting the federal or even state governments to run our local schools is a bad idea."
o D. All of the above. | If you answered D, you are correct.

A. US Dept. of Education Acting Commissioner Dr. John King. Source: http://wamc.org/post/nys-education-commissioner-discusses-common-core-troy
B. Statement made by Ted Cruz. Source: http://www.cruz.senate.gov/?p=press_release&id=1268
C. Statement by Rick Santorum. Source: *Blue Collar Conservatives*, April 28, 2014, (131–32) |

Table 4.1, part two

3. Which of the following statements were made by public figures about education reform? o A. "Now everyone will tell you nationwide, the key to education reform is a teacher evaluation system." o B. "You can either help the politically powerful unions. Or you can help the kids." o C. "[P]oliticians have continued to defend a system of tenure that is weakening the effectiveness of public education. Generations of hopelessness are being produced by this recalcitrance." o D. All of the above.	If you answered D, you are correct. A. Statement from Governor Andrew Cuomo's State of the State address. Source: http://www.saratogian.com/general-news/20150121/video-wtranscript-state-of-the-state-2015 B. Statement by Jeb Bush. Source: 2012 Republican National Convention speech, Aug 29, 2012 C. Statement made by Lawrence Lessig. Source: "Why Don't We Have Successful Schools," (65), *Republic Lost: How Money Corrupts Congress –and a Plan to Stop It*, New York, Boston: Twelve, Hatchett Group, 2011
4. Which of the following statements were actually made by public figures discussing the topic of education reform? o A. Call for the dismantling the "cartel of existing colleges and universities." o B. "Merit pay at every school in the country would create a system superior overall to what we have now. We hear all this agonizing about the criteria for merit pay, about the difficulty of deciding who deserves more.	If you answered D, you are correct. A. Phrase by Marco Rubio. Source: http://www.nytimes.com/politics/first-draft/2015/07/07/marco-rubio-attacks-higher-education-cartel-and-jabs-rivals/. By Jeremy W. Peters *New York Times*, First Draft, July 7, 2015 B. Statements by Mike Huckabee. Source: ABC This Week 2013 series of 2016 presidential hopefuls, Oct 20, 2013 C. Statements by Hillary Clinton. Source: http://www.publiccharters.org/wp-content/uploads/2014/04/Who-Supports-Charter-Schools.pdf

Table 4.1, part three

The truth is that principals know who their best teachers are." o C. "I stand behind the charter school/public school movement, because parents do deserve greater choice within the public school system to meet the unique needs of their children. Slowly but surely, we're beginning to create schooling opportunities through the public school charter system-raising academic standards, empowering educators." o D. All of the above.	
5. Which statements about education were made by public figures running for national office? o A. "I honestly think we don't need a Department of Education." o B. "Our public school system is log jammed, broken-down, paralyzed . . . and it's been unable to reform itself. That's because it's beyond fixing, I'm afraid. I'm not just talking about schools in our inner cities; the problem runs to our small towns as well, and all across the country." o C. "This is a time of educational crisis. . . . There isn't one place in the country where we can say the graduation rate is high enough." o D. All of the above.	If you answered D, you are correct. A. Statements by Marco Rubio. Source: *AP*, By Michelle Rindels. Posted: 09/02/2015 10:38 AM EDT Huff Post Education B. Statements by John Kasich. Source: *Los Angeles Times*, "Kasich Eagerly Rolls", 4/6/99, Apr 6, 1999; *Stand for Something*, by John Kasich, p.176–178 , May 10, 2006 C. Statement by former US Department of Education Secretary Arne Duncan on "Ineffective Teachers." Source: vimeo.com

Table 4.1, part four

NOTE

1. John Cassidy, "John Angus Deaton: A Skeptical Optimist Wins the Economics Nobel" *New Yorker* (September 7, 2015), accessed September 7, 2015, http://www.newyorker.com/news/john-cassidy/angus-deaton-a-skeptical-optimist-wins-the-economics-nobel.

FIVE

Tales Told by Idiots Signifying Nothing

The title of William Faulkner's novel *The Sound and the Fury*, which he drew from and as allusion to Shakespeare's *Macbeth*, provides the framework for our examination of some political policymakers who make a great many pronouncements and determinations without a full understanding of children, actual classrooms, and situations in public schools.

"According to sociologists who study these events, in a moral panic," states educator and writer Dana Goldstein in her book *The Teacher Wars*, "policy makers and the media focus on a single class of people (in our case, veteran public school teachers) as emblems of a larger, complex social problem (socioeconomic inequality, as evidenced by achievement gaps)."[1] If, however, policymakers do not recognize or acknowledge the larger social issues, they are likely to make decisions that are harmful rather than helpful. This approach is something akin to putting a Band-Aid on a gushing wound.

Using the conceit of a perfect storm, we could follow the rhetoric of politicians, business leaders, and the media that have taken press releases from businesses and politicians to promote a specific agenda, resulting in destructive forces. This convergence is about the coming of not just any storm but the confluence of tornado, hurricane, flooding, high and low pressure collisions, torrential rains, and severe lightning descending upon public education and school teachers.

There is little, if any, distinction made between districts and individual achievements but rather a condemnation of public education in general—the bulwark of our democracy—and the teachers who are left to be the scapegoated "causes" of this storm. Solutions offered by these policymakers are without nuance, which a meaningful reform would suggest is necessitated.

We simultaneously demand teachers prepare students for business, for careers in businesses, and then vote for politicians who represent business interests, with businesses outsourcing American companies, eliminating the very positions for which students were "prepared" to compete. The current catchphrase in public education is that students must be "college and career ready" for engineering jobs, yet those American companies hiring engineers are known to turn down qualified American engineer applicants in favor of candidates from India, Pakistan, and other places in the world where salaries are lower.

What is the real motivation behind those directing the current education reform movement? A more penetrating examination reveals very different motivations than helping children learn.

Lee Fang, in an article entitled "Venture Capitalists Are Poised to 'Disrupt' Everything about the Education Market," discusses the imposing size of the education market and why businesses and politicians are suddenly so very interested in "reforming" education: "Venture capitalists and for-profit firms are salivating over the exploding $788.7 billion market in K–12 education."[2] Education in these terms is intended only as a means to the ends of acquiring capital.

We should be asking if the motives of politicians and business leaders directing education policy are suspect, if not overtly, then implicitly, and ethically compromised. Fang quotes business executives who are transparent here about their motives: "'It's [public money for education] really the last honeypot for Wall Street,' says Donald Cohen, the executive director of In the Public Interest, a think tank that tracks the privatization of roads, prisons, schools and other parts of the economy."[3]

Fang further notes, "The GSV paper calls for reformers to join the 'education battlefield' (A colorful diagram depicts 'unions' and 'status quo' forces equipped with muskets across businesses and other 'change agents' equipped with a fighter jet and a howitzer.)"[4] This diagram is not a data-driven measurement, as it at first appears to be, but an editorial in the form of a graphic with unions pitifully holding outdated weapons while the businesses are equated with fighter jets; the violence of the imagery also shows the propensity for business to use terms and symbols associated with violence.

Politicians and business people adopting a mocking and condescending tone and approach toward teachers and teachers' unions are evident in the language and even the symbols (muskets versus fighter jets). By using the words of these business leaders, Fang allows them to expose their real interest in education reform: "we [in the GVS paper] believe the opportunity to build numerous multi-billion-dollar education enterprises is finally real."[5] This reform is not about children or their education; it is about making money in an area that may now be "mined."

"Follow the money," was Deep Throat's secretly whispered advice to reporter Bob Woodward, who was investigating the Watergate scandal of the Nixon presidency. It is now common knowledge that the money followed a trail from the Watergate burglars to G. Gordon Liddy to Howard Hunt, and the eventual discoveries led all the way to the White House and Richard Nixon. At the time, however, this information was a closely guarded secret. These revelations were dangerous in 1972. Taking on the moneyed interests can be a dangerous proposition at any point in our history as well.

Following the money in education reform today should give everyone pause, if not grave concern. A documentary by Colorado filmmaker and teacher Brian Malone follows the trail of business and politics into "education reform." His film *Education, Inc.* examines the "free-market and for-profit interests that have been quietly and systematically privatizing America's public education system under the banner of 'school choice,'" according to the documentary's website.[6] After producing the movie that questioned the motives of the moneyed powers, Malone lost his job teaching in one school district where the school board election was heavily influenced by these business interests.

Businesses and politicians on both sides of the political aisle are tied to enormous profits from selling new testing and setting up charter schools. Is anyone in government questioning the value of these practices that are making the policymakers more money? Kids are not products, so allowing business to dictate public education curricula, models, policies, and practices is indeed frightening, especially with their track record.

After all, a defective product is thrown away in business, factories set up overseas for cheaper labor, often with children making the items because no child labor laws govern these factories. The business model has no moral compass except to make money, so how and why is the business model the arbiter of all things that must change in education?

In his dissent to the Citizens United recent ruling in the Supreme Court, Justice John Paul Stevens wrote (with whom Justice Ginsburg, Justice Breyer, and Justice Sotomayor join, concurring in part and dissenting in part), "A Government captured by corporate interests, they may come to believe, will be neither responsive to their needs nor willing to give their views a fair hearing."[7]

He further clarified the concept that corporations are not, in fact, people: "[C]orporations have no consciences, no beliefs, no feelings, no thoughts, no desires. . . . [T]hey are not themselves members of 'We the People' by whom and for whom our Constitution was established."[8] Although Justice Stevens was addressing the topic of the Citizens United legislation in his dissent, his words about corporations apply here as well, in that corporations have no "beliefs, no feelings, no thoughts, no desires" about children's education. They are formed to make money.

In the political comments about education, the overwhelming lack of understanding of many aspects of public education is transparent to teachers and students, but perhaps less so to the general public.

When career politician and Ohio Governor John Kasich made the following pronouncement, many in the media printed it as if the comment was worthy of meaningful discussion. "Why shouldn't teachers have to compete for the right to educate students?" questioned Kasich in *Stand for Something: The Battle for America's Soul*.[9]

Battling for America's soul, Kasich and other politicians should be aware that teachers actually face tremendous competition in something called the job interview. One education blogger in response to the news article, "New Jersey grads in search of teaching jobs face grim market," reported that 1,200 applications were received for one teaching position.[10]

It is increasingly difficult to find teaching employment for qualified applicants because of the fierce competition from not only new professionals entering the field but from teachers who have been laid off as budget cuts got deeper. Administrators were forced to look to staffing in order to reach their bottom line.

Of course, it is easier to battle for America's soul if there is a ready-made scapegoat, and everything seems to be reduced to extreme positions. Although public education has long been under attack, as Goldstein pointed out in *The Teacher Wars*, the recent storm in the political arena—that ends up informing the culture, seems more concentrated and purposefully targeted: take down unions and teachers who support them.

Book author Alec MacGillis, in his article "Testing Time: Jeb Bush's Educational Experiment," appearing in the *New Yorker*, wrote, "According to Jim Warford, a county school superintendent in North Florida, whom Bush selected to be his K–12 school chancellor in 2003, 'He saw the teachers' unions as one of the foundations of the Democratic Party, and he saw a great advantage—that anything he could do to undercut the teachers' union would have a political return."[11]

Bush's former ally, Warford, makes the politics behind this "reform" abundantly clear: take down unions and their political voice. If this, rather than improving students' educational opportunities, is the agenda, then it is disturbing. It should also be made transparent to the general public. When we make policy, the agendas must be clear.

Separating out people who actually want to improve schools from strictly political and business interests is very difficult. While we must consider that there are well-meaning people in politics and business who really want to better students' performances in sciences and mathematics, the trail, unfortunately, leads back to decisions being made that, too frequently, involve agendas other than education for kids.

To return to the storm metaphor, hurricane winds in the form of illogical and contradictory statements from politicians, debris clouds made up of confusing "professional development" (see "Menu" in chapter 8), a meeting of high and low pressure fronts of long work days without adequate preparation time, and the stress of high stakes testing on students and teachers have converged on American public schools.

We could continue this conceit, bringing flooding from heavy rain in the form of children's drug abuse, poverty, unstable home lives, and lost jobs and opportunities in America. Lightning storms only complicate the scene with rapid changes in administration, changing emphasis and policies. Prevailing winds suggest public education as the bulwark of democracy is on shaky grounds.

Just as in Donald Barthelme's story "The School,"[12] this narrative of education reform increases in severity, even as it accelerates into absurdity. Will Americans recognize this downward spiral in time to prevent further damage to one of the foundations of our democracy—our public education?

NOTES

1. Dana Goldstein, *The Teacher Wars: A History of America's Most Embattled Profession* (New York: Anchor Books, Division of Random House, 2015), 5–6.

2. Lee Fang, "Venture Capitalists Are Poised to 'Disrupt' Everything about the Education Market," *The Nation* (September 25, 2014), accessed September 15, 2015, http://www.thenation.com/article/venture-capitalists-are-poised-disrupt-everything-about-education-market/.

3. Fang, "Venture Capitalists Are Poised to 'Disrupt.'"

4. Ibid.

5. Ibid.

6. Brian Malone, *Education, Inc. For Profit. For Kids?* Fast Forward Films, Master script transcript, 2015.

7. Justice John Paul Stevens, Dissenting opinion in the Citizens United ruling, Legal Information Institute, Cornell University Law School, *Citizens United v. Federal Election Comm'n* (No. 08-205), (January 21, 2010), accessed October 6, 2015, https://www.law.cornell.edu/supct/html/08-205.ZX.html.

8. Ibid.

9. John Kasich, *Stand for Something: The Battle for America's Soul* (New York: Grand Central Publishing, Hachette Group, 2007), 176–77.

10. Kathleen O'Brien, "New Jersey Grads in Search of Teaching Jobs Face Grim Market" NJ Advance Media for NJ.com (May 9, 2010), accessed October 20, 2015, http://www.nj.com/news/index.ssf/2010/05/newly-graduated_aspiring_teach.html.

11. Alec MacGillis, "Testing Time: Jeb Bush's Educational Experiment," *New Yorker*, January 26, 2015.

12. Donald Barthelme, "The School," Blogspot. *Wandering about Short Fiction*, accessed November 10, 2015, http://dentfictionworkshop.blogspot.com/2013/08/donald-barthelmes-school.html.

SIX

Why Teacher Evaluations Tied to Tests Don't Work

After launching the country into Race to the Top, which felt surprisingly like former President Bush's and Senator Ted Kennedy's No Child Left Behind legislation[1] in a number of aspects, President Obama turned away from some of the very measures that defined this US Education Department policy directive. President Obama's more recent statements, in "An Open Letter to America's Parents and Teachers: Let's Make Our Testing Smarter," shift from the focus on testing, as shown in this quotation that appeared in his blog on *Huffington Post* on October 28, 2015:

> But when I look back on the great teachers who shaped my life, what I remember isn't the way they prepared me to take a standardized test. What I remember is the way they taught me to believe in myself. To be curious about the world. To take charge of my own learning so that I could reach my full potential. They inspired me to open up a window into parts of the world I'd never thought of before.[2]

Not so strangely, these statements echo the sentiments of most teachers and administrators, who felt that way long before the federal legislation. While then President Obama's sentiments in his letter to America are to be lauded, he did little here to remove the mandates that link a teacher's job to his or her students' test scores. We are still left with that "accountability" measurement that is, more than anything, simply arbitrary.

Since that announcement, Obama signed Every Student Succeeds Act (ESSA) into law, and this bipartisan legislation may reverse some of the damage from Race to the Top. But even with that caveat, many schools around the country have already bought testing, set up the mandated testing practices and procedures, and moved ahead with implementing the Common Core, tying testing to teachers' jobs.

After all of the time and money put into trying to meet the mandates, these testing practices and procedures, as well as the implementation of the Common Core curricula, will not be easily discarded. In other words, policy directives remain with us often long after everyone has lost faith in the outcomes. Even when policy changes, we are still in the position of having to deal with previous policies.

Perhaps this next statement from the US Department of Education's "Testing Action Plan" is most troubling because it leaves the "accountability" of a teacher's livelihood still tied to test scores while "recommending" that less class time be spent in test preparation: "Second, tests shouldn't occupy too much classroom time, or crowd out teaching and learning."[3]

Teachers' positions may still be linked to their students' scores, but much less time is to be spent preparing them for the very measures that will determine the teacher's livelihood—like the infamous Catch 22.

While it is early to determine whether or not the bipartisan legislation on education passed by Congress—Every Student Succeeds Act (ESSA)—can offer more successes in improving education, it is not too early to point out the fact that, once again, the same top-down formulas are going to be applied. The fact that both sides of the political aisle recognized a need to change some aspects of federal legislation on education policy is, however, encouraging.

State governors, teachers' union leadership, school administrators, and parents worked behind the scenes to encourage this reform. The Bipartisan Policy Center's Governors' Council's conference report was introduced to Congress by senators Lamar Alexander (R-TN), Patty Murray (D-WA), and House of Representative congressmen John Kline (R-MN) and Robert Scott (D-VA).[4] In addition to the primary architects of the legislation named, senators Dean Heller (R-NV) and Joe Manchin (D-WV) are credited with authoring the aspect of the bill that gives "governors a stronger role in the development of the state education plan."[5]

While the bipartisan effort in Congress and by governors is to be commended, problems in education reform not only remain but are actually compounded by ESSA. Whether the federal or state government is dictating policy, classroom educators' voices seem to be marginalized. "Localizing" is not generally including the most important voices in reform processes. In addition, the concept of national oversight in terms of curriculum is lost here, and expectations, curricula offering, and academic objectives for students are likely to vary widely from state to state.

Were some educators' and parents' concerns—as well as the governors' voices—heard, resulting in ESSA legislation? Yes. In fact, parents and their children refusing to take the required summative assessments were likely the largest driving force behind the reform of Race to the Top. The revolt here caused legislators to rethink their positions.

Yet, in the US Department of Education's Testing Action Plan, admission of error is coupled with laying the burden on teachers' backs: "In too many schools, there is unnecessary testing and not enough clarity of purpose applied to the task of assessing students, consuming too much instructional time and creating undue stress for educators and students. The Administration bears some of the responsibility for this, and we are committed to being part of the solution."[6]

While it is comforting that the "Administration" accepts "some" of the responsibility, many of the problems caused by the legislation remain. Admitting error is, again, laudable, but not a panacea. Part of the "solution," does not remove student test scores as a measure of whether or not a teacher is able to keep his or her job. In the December 2015 issue of the *New York Times*, the Associated Press reports that the new ESSA legislation appears to still contain the testing requirements.[7]

Whether or not the most recently passed federal education law—ESSA—will have positive effects on student outcomes, many of the same problems created by Race to the Top and No Child Left Behind remain. Largely illogical testing issues in public education will, it seems, remain in the political sphere and continue to determine teachers' employment and lives.

Providing historical context for the puzzling, but often adamant, systematic attacks on teachers from both political parties and the public, Dana Goldstein wrote in *The Teacher Wars*:

> According to sociologists who study these events, in a moral panic, policy makers and the media focus on a single class of people (in our case, veteran public school teachers) as emblems of a large, complex social problem (socioeconomic inequality, as evidenced by educational achievement gaps).[8]

These wars on teachers are economic, policy, and legislation driven, and very political.

Certain political figures have made their platforms around education "reform," and those platforms, terminology, and ideology will remain with us long after the politician ceases to be in the public eye. Former Florida governor, Jeb Bush, in a public pronouncement on education, stated, "So I think we need to go in a completely different approach . . . [education] will be a market-oriented approach to align what we want."[9] The phrases "market-approach" and "align what we want" are indicators that students' interests are not what come first here.

What is critically important to recognize here is not the politician who stated the words, but the words themselves. When we accept the approach to our children's education as a market approach, we are heading down a dangerous slope. Too often, politicians serve other interest groups.

Under the largely political assault on education, public school teachers are repeatedly disparaged, and the test makers and charter school industries move in, bashing and smashing as they go, destroying all that works, without real analysis of what does or does not work so well. This happens, partially, because research and analysis are time-consuming, and there seems to be a political will to "fix it" immediately.

Returning to the concept of tying teachers' positions to students' test scores, educators and psychologists have long pointed out the fact that punishments do not yield the best results. Writer Dana Goldstein makes a point of not focusing on one political party for laying out the causes of this disastrous "reform" movement: "In the Obama era, the predominant policy response to these very real problems has been a narrow one: to weaken teachers' tenure protections and then use measures of student learning—a euphemism for children's scores on an ever-expanding battery of hastily designed tests—to identify and fire bad teachers."[10]

Supposedly, these tests were intended to measure "value added" by the teacher or VAMs (value-added measurements). The silly formula is as ridiculous to teachers as it is to students and anyone who takes the time to determine how it all adds up. At one point, the mathematics teachers interviewed looked at the VAM formulas designed to determine whether or not a teacher could keep his or her job. They discovered that there was no way to actually make the math work. That is right: it did not add up. While politically expedient—as long as no one is looking carefully or asking any questions—the VAM scores may be used in any fashion desired by people both inside and outside of education.

Because policymakers are so far removed from actual classrooms, it is easy to see how they could come up with decisions about measuring student performance to determine the value of an individual teacher. Logic would seem to dispel any notion of tying students' scores to measures of teacher effectiveness, but reasoning has not prevailed here.

First, a summative test given on one day introduces so many variables with possible outcomes, suggesting the difficulty of accurate measurement. The chances of the results being indicative of the student's optimal performance are poor in many cases.

One test does not measure the child's capability or the teacher's ability, only where that child is on one given day with a myriad of variables in play. Even imagining optimal conditions for every student, we are left with many classrooms of struggling students in a very good teacher's room, and high achieving students in an ineffective teacher's classroom. In other words, the test does not measure the teacher's performance. In many cases, the test does not measure the student's learning.

Examining how these tests are conducted, administered, and interpreted to count for or against teachers is a chapter in itself, but to summarize the problem: there is no consistency within districts let alone between school districts, between states, between wealthy districts and poorer districts. There is a tremendous amount of subjectivity built into the process of this seemingly impartial arbiter of measurement.

In one district, a teacher's scores were "curved" to bring her up, while other teachers' scores in her own department were not curved. By way of another example of an interviewed educator: one teacher had a roster with students who were chronically absent but still technically in her class. Those chronically absent students were dropped from her rolls; yet another teacher in the same district had her chronically absent students count against her "impartial" Annual Professional Performance Review (APPR) measurement score.

The application of the APPR evaluation has been flawed and inconsistent within schools, let alone between schools and between states, from the outset. However, the federal and state governments' initiatives were intended to be carried out, mandates still allowed room for skewed scoring, and imperfect scoring permits arbitrary decisions to be made.

When policymakers discuss "data-driven" results, we should note that much of the data obtained is compromised from the outset by the processes, the testing, imbalances in classrooms, and a host of socioeconomic factors. The reality does not fit neatly into a VAM formula, so the reality of what children and teachers face on a daily basis appears to be simply discarded.

Another example could be found in an interview with a teacher who had six students who did not show up for the final assessment test. Six zeros were factored into her APPR evaluation. In the case of two of the students in that group, the teacher had seen them a total of five times during the entire course. The teacher's VAM was determined based upon children she had no ability to help or affect in any way.

Why or how could that happen? It is possible to get around the "system" in multiple ways. Although students are considered dropouts after an extended time out of school, they need only show up one day to restart the count. Because attendance figures into social services to families and children, as well, some individuals have figured out how to continue to get benefits and not really attend school—just have it appear as if they are attending.

Teachers—who have the good fortune—will have course loads that are lighter and rosters of students who are high achieving with parents as partners in education. Course loads in one department in one district varied from a number of thirty-six students for one teacher to 112 for another teacher in the same department. Other teachers have students on their rolls with troubled academic pasts, resulting in far fewer contacts with the students due to absences, detentions, and suspensions.

In other words, the idea that teachers are, in any way, being fairly measured through this type of testing is an absolute absurdity. It is hard to imagine any profession—other than teaching—that would permit such an obviously unfair evaluation system to jeopardize job security. Here again, politics played an oversized roll in both creating and sustaining the unfairness. Attacks on unions, to some extent, held unions back from more vigorously defending their members: the classroom teachers.

Well-known educator and writer Nancie Atwell recently told a PBS *News Hour* correspondent that, "Anybody's achievement is driven by interest."[11] It is Atwell's well-documented and validated concept that "students will invest in their learning if there is a real curiosity and passion."[12] This logical and common-sense statement makes so much sense that it is almost certain not to find its way into education reform policy under the current direction. PBS news reporter April Brown noted that Atwell does not "believe in tests and quizzes." Atwell elaborates:

> When we evaluate our students, it's on the basis of portfolios of their work, and students self-assess as part of the portfolio process. They answer questions on every discipline about what they have been thinking, doing, learning. It's a question not of being accountable to the state, but of being accountable to our students' parents.[13]

Yet the fallacy persists in political and government circles that testing will somehow produce better results. A quick examination of only a few of these mitigating factors makes it readily apparent that tying a teacher's job to student scores is not only unfair but ludicrous. What other profession would permit their colleagues to be fired for reasons that were completely outside of their purview or ability to control?

Let us be thoughtful and consider the various factors in children's lives that affect how well they learn outside of the reach of the classroom. In his article "A World without Work" that appears in the *Atlantic*, Derek Thompson examines Youngstown, Ohio, as a model of where things went wrong and how "the end of work" changed the culture:

> Youngstown was transformed not only by an economic disruption but also by a psychological and cultural breakdown. Depression, spousal abuse, and suicide all became much more prevalent; the caseload of the area's mental-health center tripled within a decade [after the steel mills closed down]. The city built four prisons in the mid-1990s—a rare growth industry.[14]

We need policymakers to walk into classrooms and stay for more than five minutes—in the following scenario, a high school classroom—with their eyes and ears open. While the story may seem like an exaggeration to those who have never actually spent any time in classrooms and gotten to know the students, it is a truer picture of various situations of students than the abstract and idealized one policymakers tend to envision or have manufactured.

STORY OF TEST DAY

Jennifer arrives seven minutes late, tugging at her too short skirt. She is pregnant but has not told her mother or her boyfriend who, the girl believes, is already seeing another student.

Also late is Ricky, whose father recently lost his job and decided not to come home last night. His mother was crying when Ricky left her in the kitchen with a table covered in unpaid bills.

Susan walks in talking condescendingly to her peers, much to their annoyance. A high-functioning autistic, she conceives of brilliant insights that float above the level of most students in the class, but she frequently exists in a world in which she feels like the only inhabitant. Because she sees many ways of examining a problem, she typically runs out of time on standardized tests. She is, however, prepared to take the test, nervous and expectant, worried that her scores will not reflect her intelligence—which they will not.

Sean lost his mother to cancer a few weeks ago, and he is back in school but withdrawn. He looks at Susan with incredulity. His first serious girlfriend dropped him a short time before his mother's death, and he is struggling to come to school, to read, listen, and think—even to respond.

David, who is homeless since his stepfather kicked him out, is only nine minutes late because he knew there was a test, so he did his best, but he had to bum a ride from Jeff who is not even his friend. David was camping out in the backyard of his ex-girlfriend's house until her father found out, but this is his third house in a week, and he isn't sure where he will be able to crash tonight.

Across the room, Miranda is transitioning sexes, at war with herself, her family, and some of her friends. She hates her mother because her mother told her that she would "get over it," and her father left years ago, so there is no parent and no friend to whom she feels connected.

Two desks in front of Miranda, John is nodding off, mixing a concoction of downers, experimenting in chemistry on his body before and after school, and as some students say, "why do you think he has to go to the bathroom so often?"

The pretty girl in front of him feels she is unnoticed and is secretly cutting herself in places that don't show. Sometimes she winces at strange and inappropriate times.

The 250-pound boy across from her keeps staring at pretty Mary, but she never looks at him because he has a severe case of acne in addition to being tremendously overweight. Because the water was recently shut off in his mother's apartment, he hasn't had a shower in days. He has never had a girlfriend and can think about nothing else.

Samantha couldn't sleep all night because she realizes the importance of this test, and she is worried that she has not prepared sufficiently, even though she constantly studies. Her eyes hurt, and her stomach is upset—the bile already working its way up to her throat.

Jack, Bill, and Jaquan are absent a lot—Bill closing in on thirty days. Jaquan forgot he had this class today, so he is late, going to the wrong room again. Jack and Bill don't make it again today.

Marcia rubs her fingers. She has not yet been diagnosed with anorexia, the secret she harbors like a bad lover.

Tracy lost her sister over the summer to a heroin overdose. The fact that Tracy always looked up to her big sister, and that her mother is drowning her sorrow over her daughter's death in alcohol and pills, leaves her feeling isolated and scared nearly all of the time.

Jessica is sleeping with the soon-to-be-divorced father of one of her best friends and is carrying on the affair in secret, but her friend is starting to suspect something.

Greg discovered porn is easier to make than he would have believed, and he can make more money on it than as a clerk in a grocery store. He's been up all night and can't see straight.

James's cancer is in remission, but he still wears a hat to cover his baldness, attempting not to be too self-conscious. His mother says he has nothing to worry about, that the cancer will not come back, but James feels like it is his double, his shadow, waiting for the right moment to return.

Andy has been cheating for years, plagiarizing every paper. Those teachers thought they had him once, but his parents brought in a lawyer, and by the end of the meeting, his grade had been changed and the teacher sufficiently chastised for daring to accuse him of copying, even though he did. He has most tests down to a science, knows who to text, when to look like he's picking up his pen when he is checking for answers, but today has him a little concerned. No one he knows has taken this test, and it is clear that he does not know the material. He is already scanning the room to determine when and how he will lean to retrieve his dropped pen or pencil.

Mary Jane has a chronic urinary tract infection and a pass to leave class as often as she would like, multiple times each class. She knows it is her escape, because at this point she is so far behind that she feels it is pointless to try and catch up, which is also how Steve feels since his family made him come to this "stupid school" from his former home in another state where he could get top grades and do next to nothing.

Transferring in from an inner-city school, Joe's dyslexia has not yet been identified, nor has the new kid Chris's undetected vision problem.

Charlotte's grandmother has Alzheimer's, and Charlotte is afraid she will have to move to her new stepfather's house with her mother.

Bosnian immigrant Dino is nervously texting on his hidden cell phone because he is afraid he won't know the English words, even though he has already reached the limit for ESL (English as a second language) help.

Isabel is suffering from early warning signs of as-yet undiagnosed schizophrenia.

Alex borrowed some money from his parents—a lot of money—without asking, and he either lost it or a friend stole it from him. He has searched everywhere, and a trickle of sweat is rolling down his back.

Kim found out a few weeks ago that she did not get into the college of her choice. All of her hard work over the years seems to have been for nothing, and she is no longer angry because "the whole fucking thing is bullshit."

Derek has always hated Mrs. M, so he figures this is a good chance to get even, knowing his score counts little against him but could determine the fate of her career.

Azar is far more concerned about her father's absence and her mother's crying than any test in school. She wonders what she will face when she gets home.

Anthony returned from an out-of-school suspension for having just a few joints in his locker, and he is "pissed because this place is a fuckin' prison."

Cassandra knows that the test will not count against her, only her teacher. Cassie has never liked her teacher because the first day she called her "Cassie" as if she was familiar.

Kelsey won't be coming to school today or any other day again because she killed herself last week. Even though she almost never came to school, the entire classroom is reeling from hearing about her death.

"Good morning." Their teacher just brought in the state LAT (summary assessment test) and is handing out materials to her class. Test directions are read. There are audible coughs, shifting in chairs.

"Good luck, kids. Concentrate. Do your best." Your teacher's job depends on it.

All of the names of the students have been changed, but each fictitious name represents a real person who passed through an actual public school teacher's classroom.

NOTES

1. Claudia Wallis, "No Child Left Behind: Doomed to Fail?" "Kennedy's Top Ten Legislative Battles," *Time* (June 8, 2008), accessed January 1, 2016, http://content.time.com/time/specials/packages/article/0,28804,1918873_1918869_1918857,00.html

2. President Barack Obama, "An Open Letter to America's Parents and Teachers: Let's Make Our Testing Smarter," *The Huffington Post*, The Blog, HuffPost Politics (October 28, 2015), accessed October 28, 2015, http://www.huffingtonpost.com/barack-obama/an-open-letter-to-americas-parents-and-teachers_b_8392692.html.

3. "Fact Sheet: Testing Action Plan," US Department of Education (October 24, 2015), accessed October 27, 2015, http://www.ed.gov/news/press-releases/fact-sheet-testing-action-plan.

4. Bipartisan Policy Center, (December 9, 2015), accessed December 12, 2015, http://bipartisanpolicy.org/press-release/former-govs-essa-returns-power-on-education-to-states/.

5. Ibid.

6. "Fact Sheet: Testing Action Plan."

7. Julie Hirschfeld, "President Obama Signs into Law a Rewrite of No Child Left Behind," *New York Times* (December 2, 2015), accessed December 10, 2015, http://www.nytimes.com/2015/12/11/us/politics/president-obama-signs-into-law-a-rewrite-of-no-child-left-behind.html.

8. Goldstein, *The Teacher Wars*, 5–6.

9. Bush, Top Ten First Tier debate, transcript.

10. Goldstein, *Teacher Wars*, 2.

11. Nancie Atwell, "'World's Best Teacher' Does Not Believe in Tests and Quizzes," PBS *News Hour* (Interview on April 29, 2015), accessed August 17, 2015, http://www.pbs.org/newshour/bb/worlds-best-teacher-believe-tests-quizzes/.

12. Atwell, "World's Best Teacher."

13. Ibid.

14. Derek Thompson, "A World without Work," *Atlantic* (Vol. 316, No. 1, July/August, 2015), 51–61.

SEVEN
What Hurt

Before we make and enact policy, we need to much more fully consider what public schools, administrators, teachers, and students face on a daily basis. The following is a story that is both fiction and nonfiction in the sense that it is a narrative but reveals the life stories behind the very hard lives of some students. This is a story about two students, Katherine LaFarge—who narrates her story—and Taneesha Rollins,* who try to raise their sons while still attending high school.

One year all the girls in class were pregnant, except Samantha and Chloe who already had their babies. Chloe's kid was a year and a-half at the start of the semester, so she had the toughest time getting to school regularly due to trying to find babysitters, at least ones who were not also on those lists they passed out at the end of 4th block—cause there is such a damn high ratio of kid molesters to kids in our town that it almost seems like "pervert" is a regular job. And what, with her mom still working through her drug habit and not really working all that hard at it, we only saw Chloe in school once every few weeks, if that.

Sam said she was lucky 'cause Janice—her mother—agreed to watch baby Josh if Sam didn't marry the "stupid, good-for-nothing fucker" who knocked her up, which was a no-brainer 'cause there was no way she would have married Ben, even if he managed to get a job at Wegmans, even if he stopped smoking who knows what shit he was into now, so you could see how it was hard for Sam to believe that she'd been so out of it to let him put his hands down her pants, let alone fuck her, but then again, she admitted she was pretty out of it that night.

If you ask her now, she'll say she's okay with it all 'cause she has little Josh to love and, what the fuck, that one night was fuckin' great even if her mother told her, "If you end up like me, I swear, I'll kill you with my own two hands," and Sam said she just laughed and asked Janice if she ever planned on killing her, "with her own one hand."

Janice said, "Don't you try and make a fuckin' joke out of this cause I swear," and then Sam said, "Well, swear away, Janice, 'cause I got 'one in the oven' as you used to say." So Janice dropped to her knees—all dramatic like—started moaning, until Sam said, "C'mon, Janice, let's not be so fuckin' dramatic all the time" when, surprisingly, Janice straightened up and said, "Oh, hell, what you gonna name the kid?" and "Is it a boy or girl?" Wondering if the kid was destined to carry on their tradition.

Sam said, "Boy, so at least he—," but Janice interrupted, as usual, and said, "Well, sure he can, but we won't necessarily know about all the little shits he's got running around." Then they both laughed, Sam said, "cause that seemed better than bawling," but her mother got moodier after that, until finally, Sam had to move out, too, and, at this point, she's living in Syracuse with some dude I don't know, and I'm not sure if Sam really does either.

Then when I told my mom, who I'll call LaFarge because we've been on a formal basis since birth, "The good news first: I scored 25 points higher on my SLO and LAT summatives than my baselines."

LaFarge just said, "Good Christ, what the hell is that?" I tried to explain that, "Mrs. Morenus said we," but LaFarge yelled, "Mrs. What-the-Fuck?" "Morēnus," I said, a little hesitant 'cause I could already see where she was going with this, and it had nothing to do with me doing a decent job on some random tests.

"No, not More-Anus," said LaFarge, "You've got to be kiddin' me cause no teacher could survive with that name in a roomful of boys."

"Well, she's lucky," I said, "'cause we're all girls in her room this year. All the boys got Richards."

Mrs. LaFarge smacked the kitchen table where she was sitting and yelled, "Dicks? Really? What's wrong with these people?"

"Who?" I asked even though I knew LaFarge was talking about our teachers.

"These idiot teachers you got," says LaFarge, "You don't go into a high school class with a name like Dick or More-anus." Then she heard the bad news and told me to get the hell out, that she wasn't about to raise no more babies, even though she only raised me and my brother 'cause her other two kids got given away before I even knew them, and she said that I should've been grateful I wasn't one of the ones given up, but I don't consider myself all that lucky, I said on the way out her door.

I decided to leave off the part about LaFarge calling me a slut—which went on and on until I couldn't hear her 'cause I was too far down the street—but then I got it into my head to walk all the way to Taneesha's, who'd already had her baby and got herself an apartment that her aunt helped her find 'cause Taneesha's mother was long gone with no forwarding address, and her brother got killed last year in the city by some random shooting.

"So," I said, "I'll help with baby Deelon 'til mine comes due—even after, really, cause I can take one shift," and then Taneesha the other when she gets home from school cause she's almost done with high school, even with her missing all that time when she got so sick from that infection and then being pregnant and all.

Then Deelon getting one ear ache after another and needing tubes in his ears, poor little guy, and her teachers saying that wasn't a legal excuse for absence, but I told Tee that it was legal enough, and I told her about Mrs. Morenus telling me that I should go to college, and I tried not to laugh at the time, but now I'm taking it more seriously even though I got a dozen friends who went to community college for a semester before dropping out and leaving with nothing but a big fat debt they're not gonna pay.

But I didn't say none of that to Mrs. Morenus, who told me I could write even though my grammar and mechanics need more work, and she said it in a way that made me feel kind of proud after I handed in my essay about that guy Barthelme, I think, who wrote a story I liked called "The School" 'cause things kept getting worse and worse in his story, but you were still laughing at least on the inside all the way up to the part where kids start dying.

I told Morenus that it kind of reminded me of my life, and she didn't give me a lecture or tell me what to do, but I think she was trying not to cry, so I told a lie to make her feel better, and that I was going to go to college and make a good life.

But since that day I lied, I been thinking about just taking one course at a time 'cause I'd really like to try and make my baby's life better, so Taneesha and me start planning—when we got a few minutes—which is never—but then I said that we'd make it work, and Tee believed me 'cause I can be damn convincing. We both stopped drinking, almost at least, and only smoke a little weed when her ex comes round and drops it off—like that's taking care of things for her and Deelon.

One night the other day, I was holding Deelon 'til my arms and back ached 'cause he's heavier than he looks, and he finally fell asleep after crying about half the day, when Tee comes home and kisses his forehead, touches his little fat cheek.

"Thanks, K," says Taneesha, cause she always calls me K instead of Katherine. We hug and then got to talking about our sons and how we loved them to death and want to help them grow up strong and smart and maybe, someday, if things just go right once in a while, they become the goddamn fuckin' managers of a Wegmans or maybe a lawyer or something.

*Names are fictitious and not intended to be the real names of actual students.

EIGHT
Public Education Paradigm Shifts Menu

Myths about education and teaching persist in the current rounds of political/public discourse on education "reform." One of the most dominant fictions involves the resistance of teachers to change. Casual conversations about teacher "laziness" are overheard in grocery stores, malls, banks, and nearly every place people congregate. It is a myth born in ignorance and nurtured by politicians who are eager to connect with voters.

Even a cursory glance at a typical menu of required professional development models and/or mandates in a typical, public school district will reveal teachers are continually changing practices, frequently caught in the flux, as well as flood, of new initiatives. Although most of these programs have great value, the speed with which the requirements of these mandates and models are presented and the expectations of implementation are dizzying. In addition, too often these initiatives appear to be in conflict with one another or are contradictory.

Administrators, well-intentioned and looking for state or federal funding to keep their districts operational, are frequently searching for the right formula to meet mandates, often without sufficient time to thoroughly examine these programs or conceptual imperatives in a manner that seems logical to faculty and staff. Teachers, being human, are unable, not unwilling, to incorporate the many and rapidly changing paradigm shifts due to the number of items presented to them, as well as the number of hours in a day in which they must figure out how to implement the new focus or charge.

Within a short span of time in a typical public high school, professional development looks a lot like the following unappetizing feast in which teachers are expected to swallow every course, even when appetizers and entrees don't agree, causing indigestion and, sometimes, illness. The greatest problems found in public school professional development, as typically offered, are the lack of coordination and advanced planning, as well as the business interest motives.

Administrators are often forced to react to political pressures or state or federal mandates and, in their haste to produce "solutions," may fall short of providing clear or systematic links between new initiatives. Coupled with a failure to provide sufficient time for teachers to work through the requirements, fully understand the directives, and implement new ideas and procedures, these new initiatives may be doomed from the outset.

One thing is very clear, however, about education reform: there is a great deal of money to be made if schools are "failing." Behind initiatives loom very large corporations standing to make enormous profits if schools are required to buy into their solutions, such as publishers with big stakes in the billion-dollar industry of education.[1] Businesses have a vested interest in creating the language that is repeated—schools and teachers have failed—so that the politicians and the public accepts the language of failure as fact.

If you are a businessman with a professional development product to sell to schools in crisis, you now have a ready market worth millions of tax dollars. Nearly all of the players have invested in digital education,[2] so business is incentivized to remove teacher instruction from classrooms whether or not this educational design is more or less effective for students. The "reform" is, too often, about selling a product rather than making things work better for students.

The menu that follows represents just a few years of professional development in one typical public school district, with some of the required plans of action directly contradicting each other. How teachers are to carry out these plans or implement the directives related to these overlapping and sometimes competing proposals is largely left to individuals. While districts typically slot professional development and action team meetings into schedules, it is often as absurdly short as fifteen minutes or part of a day that consists of numerous activities with no time to implement any of the strategies or fully consider the proposals.

This bill of fare should cause readers to reconsider the problems surrounding professional development and dispel the myth that public school teachers work only from 9:00 am–3:00 pm.

Dinner Menu
You must order all of the items from every category, chew each one, and swallow everything before leaving the table. Bon Appétit!
Appetizers
David Hyerle's *Thinking Maps*
Robert Marzano's *Formative Assessment and Standards-Based Grading*

Stephen Covey's "Seven Habits of the Highly Effective People"
Cognitive Coaching^{SM}
Debra Pickering's models for issuing no grades and no homework
Project-Based Learning
Pyramid Response to Intervention: RTI, Professional Learning Communities
Blended Learning
Robyn Jackson and MindSteps

Entrées

Marzano's Common Vocabulary
Transforming School Culture
Vocabulary in Context Initiative
RTI at Work: *It's about Time: Planning Interventions and Extensions in Secondary School*, edited by Mike Mattos and Austin Buffum
STEM
Standards-Based Curricula
Franklin Covey's *The Leader in Me: Whole-School Transformation Process*
Sean Covey's *The 7 Habits of Highly Effective Teens*
Richard DuFour's Professional Learning Communities at Work™
Harvey Silver's *The Thoughtful Classroom*
21st Century Skills: Rethinking How Students Learn, edited by James A. Bellanca and Ron Brandt; contributors Rebecca DuFour et al.
How to Respond when Kids Don't Learn by Buffum, Matos, and Weber
Developing Rigor in Your Classroom
Boston University Testing and More Boston University Testing
Common Core Modules
Flipped Classrooms
Digital Classroom
Massive Open Online Course (MOOC)

Desserts*

Strategic Teacher
Building Common Assessments
Comparing Assessment Scores
Thomas R. Guskey's *On Your Mark: Challenging the Conventions of Grading and Reporting*
Lee Ann Jung's and Thomas R. Guskey's *Grading Exceptional and Struggling Learners*
*Clearly, no one has room for dessert.

NOTES

1. Tim Carmody, "Why Education Publishing Is Big Business," Business. *Wired* (January 19, 2012), accessed October 29, 2015, http://www.wired.com/2012/01/why-education-publishing-is-big-business/.

2. Carmody, "Why Education Publishing Is Big Business."

NINE

Common Core Head First

With the December 2015 passage and signing of Every Student Succeeds Act (ESSA), the Common Core became less problematic for some states, teachers, and administrators, but not others.[1] Although it appears that the Common Core will no longer be a federal mandate, individual states may retain it in whole or in part.

According to the National Forum on Information Literacy, Inc., the federal mandate ceased with ESSA: "Localizing education reform opportunities to the state level, ESSA, in essence, nullifies the implementation of a national Common Core prescription."[2] However, the Common Core is nullified only as a "national prescription." Many states will retain this curricula, while others may abandon it entirely.

Individual states may proceed to mandate—or have already mandated—the Common Core in full or in part for a number of reasons that are both sound and unsound. In addition, many school districts have already rewritten their entire curricula—at an enormous expense of time and money—in the painstaking process to align with the Common Core.

This alignment operation is arduous at best, with teachers working well beyond the "school day" to accomplish the task. These districts are not simply going to abandon curricula that were so hard fought and already worked into the basic structure of student goals and objectives, as well as the expense of ordering books and supplies to meet these new demands. It is neither feasible nor wise to simply abandon the Common Core in districts where this policy directive has been partially or fully carried out.

Yet, for all of the discussion about the horrors of the Common Core, the suggested curricula—although far too broad—are less of a problem than the tests created to supposedly measure student performance. The phrase that comes up most often, and one that politicians and business people in the market of producing these tests use, is "teacher accountability." As if there is some widely held notion that teachers were not accountable to anyone before this legislation. Teachers are only accountable to their students, their students' parents (consider the number of parent/teacher conferences held each year), their departments, vice principals, principals, curriculum directors, guidance counselors, and a line of command up to the superintendent.

There are actually some positives behind the Common Core. The idea that every school in the nation should hold up similar standards for their students is a good one. Although some of the Common Core standards are unrealistically high and not attainable for some students, the concept of lifting expectations of what students are capable of doing is a positive goal, as long as we recognize that aiming high will inevitably leave some falling short. This should not be considered failure on either the part of the students or their teachers.

We should reach for the peaks in our goalsetting, but we should also have our practice grounded in reality. The idea of asking all teachers and students across the country to reach for higher standards is, as previously stated, admirable, but was never grounded in the reality of our current educational system.

The problems with the Common Core lay with implementation, misunderstanding of the language, some of the unrealistic and unreachable expectations (for some students) in the curricula, and, at least in some states, the poorly designed and too quickly rolled out testing aligned with it. This testing was supposedly intended to measure student results and hold teachers "accountable" for their students' scores before some states had even determined what those standards should be in some subject areas, including the sciences.

It is noteworthy to find that the push for STEM schools and "accountability" testing came at the same time that curricula had not yet been written or distributed in some of the sciences. It is difficult to measure the success of an outcome when the particulars of what is being measured have not yet been figured out.

Only after students took these tests, and scores were applied to teachers' performance reviews, were errors in some of the tests discovered. Some of the test questions were determined to be poorly worded or did not reflect the designed Common Core curriculum. Some test questions were found to be outright embarrassing and silly. In other words, the testing was far more flawed than even the design of the Common Core.

Rather than halt a poor process, reexamine the tests, and consider rewriting them, the faulty process continued. Teachers in subject areas for which there was no written curriculum were told to use standards from other subject areas, even though those directions made no sense. What standards should physical education teachers use: ELA (English language arts) or mathematics? The entire process began to feel more like a political or business shell game rather than reform.

As stated previously, the curriculum templates of the Common Core ask schools to offer rigorous curricula. What exactly does "rigorous" mean? In fact, it is a relative term that when applied to an honors student has a very different connotation than when applied to a student with special needs. What rigorous looks like in an AP English Literature and Composition course is dramatically disparate from rigor in a general education class or special education room. Even within classrooms, the concept varies from student to student. Yet the Common Core and testing to measure it was mandated and applied without regard for all of the distinctions we find in actuality.

If everyone was familiar with the actual content of the Common Core, it is likely that the public would ask for a more practical approach to the goals outlined. The evidence of the recent passage of ESSA suggests that many parents were aware of the problems, even if they were not familiar with the specifics of the standards. That problem—seems to have been recognized as the Common Core—is no longer federally required. Yet school districts around the country will still be using this document because it is already established as practice.

Another aspect of the problem for school districts, even under the new ESSA regulations, is an uneven application of the Common Core across the country. As noted, some states will, undoubtedly, continue to mandate these curricula. Too much has been invested to turn the clock back and "back" to what? Regardless of how well a teacher does his or her job, there are students who will not be able to meet many of the lofty goals the Common Core establishes due to a host of other factors noted here and in other chapters of this text.

There is much political discussion about the Common Core, without a great deal of understanding about where the problems lie. It is desirable to have nationwide curricula goals for schools. After the passage of ESSA, however, we are likely to have states where the Common Core standards continue in effect, and states where far lower standards are enacted. This huge disparity in our offering to our nation's children is one of the reasons that the Common Core was necessary in the first place. Rather than remove the Common Core, the particulars and the language needed to be modified.

Many people are still unfamiliar with the exact nature of what was required by adoption of the Common Core. By way of brief overview of what it involves in just two subject areas at different points of the education spectrum, here is a summary.

One charge—in just one discipline—of the Common Core framers states English teachers choose many more "informational texts: Literary Nonfiction and Historical, Scientific, and Technical Texts."[3] During the same semester or year course, English teachers are to introduce the poetry and literature of William Shakespeare, John Keats, Charlotte Brontë, Emily Dickinson, F. Scott Fitzgerald, Zora Neale Hurston, Lorraine Hansberry, Jhumpa Lahiri (suggested).

They are to teach eleventh graders complimentary nonfiction texts, including *Common Sense* by Thomas Paine, *Walden* by Henry David Thoreau, "Society and Solitude" by Ralph Waldo Emerson, "The Fallacy of Success" by G. K. Chesterton, *Black Boy* by Richard Wright, "Politics and the English Language" by George Orwell, and "Take the Tortillas Out of Your Poetry" by Rudolfo Anaya.[4]

English teachers are asked to introduce more Shakespeare texts while, simultaneously, they are being asked to include more nonfiction and reduce the role of literature in the curriculum. The paradox is not lost on English teachers. How does one teacher add more literature while de-emphasizing literature and emphasizing nonfiction? It would appear that English teachers have to introduce many more texts as they are also supporting concepts in engineering, science, and mathematics. In addition, all of these new texts are very expensive for school districts to purchase.

Anyone familiar with any of these works that the Common Core suggests for eleventh graders will be aware of the challenges faced by students and teachers. At the same time, these English teachers are expected to support technology and STEM subjects in their classrooms. No one has yet figured out a reasonable way for all of these directives to actually be successfully carried out in a logical and timely manner.

If the Common Core is taken as a model and not a dictum, as the new ESSA legislation appears to suggest, the effects would come closer to matching the intent of some of those well-meaning individuals who are involved in the reform process. But its uneven adoption and application around the country actually make for more problems than solutions.

It is likely that most parents are unfamiliar with the actual wording of the Common Core and the testing now in place. Much of this testing and curricula will continue to be in place even after ESSA.

When members of the public criticize schools today, in comparisons to their own education, they might want to first look at a few of the requirements every high school junior and senior is expected to meet under the Common Core in just one area.

Here is an excerpt taken directly from the Common Core in English, high school level:

Craft and Structure:
CCSS.ELA-Literacy.RL.11-12.4
Determine the meaning of words and phrases as they are used in the text, including figurative and connotative meanings; analyze the impact of specific word choices on meaning and tone, including words with

multiple meanings or language that is particularly fresh, engaging, or beautiful. (Include Shakespeare as well as other authors.)

CCSS.ELA-Literacy.RL.11-12.5
Analyze how an author's choices concerning how to structure specific parts of a text (e.g., the choice of where to begin or end a story, the choice to provide a comedic or tragic resolution) contribute to its overall structure and meaning as well as its aesthetic impact.

CCSS.ELA-Literacy.RL.11-12.6
Analyze a case in which grasping a point of view requires distinguishing what is directly stated in a text from what is really meant (e.g., satire, sarcasm, irony, or understatement).

CCSS.ELA-Literacy.RL.11-12.7
Analyze multiple interpretations of a story, drama, or poem (e.g., recorded or live production of a play or recorded novel or poetry), evaluating how each version interprets the source text. (Include at least one play by Shakespeare and one play by an American dramatist.)

CCSS.ELA-Literacy.RL.11-12.9
Demonstrate knowledge of eighteenth-, nineteenth- and early-twentieth-century foundational works of American literature, including how two or more texts from the same period treat similar themes or topics.

Writing:
CCSS.ELA-Literacy.W.11-12.1.b
Develop claim(s) and counterclaims fairly and thoroughly, supplying the most relevant evidence for each while pointing out the strengths and limitations of both in a manner that anticipates the audience's knowledge level, concerns, values, and possible biases.

CCSS.ELA-Literacy.W.11-12.1.c
Use words, phrases, and clauses as well as varied syntax to link the major sections of the text, create cohesion, and clarify the relationships between claim(s) and reasons, between reasons and evidence, and between claim(s) and counterclaims.

CCSS.ELA-Literacy.W.11-12.2
Write informative/explanatory texts to examine and convey complex ideas, concepts, and information clearly and accurately through the effective selection, organization, and analysis of content.

CCSS.ELA-Literacy.W.11-12.2.b

Develop the topic thoroughly by selecting the most significant and relevant facts, extended definitions, concrete details, quotations, or other information and examples appropriate to the audience's knowledge of the topic.

CCSS.ELA-Literacy.W.11-12.2.d

Use precise language, domain-specific vocabulary, and techniques such as metaphor, simile, and analogy to manage the complexity of the topic.

CCSS.ELA-Literacy.W.11-12.3

Write narratives to develop real or imagined experiences or events using effective technique, well-chosen details, and well-structured event sequences.

CCSS.ELA-Literacy.W.11-12.3.b

Use narrative techniques, such as dialogue, pacing, description, reflection, and multiple plot lines, to develop experiences, events, and/or characters.

CCSS.ELA-Literacy.W.11-12.3.c

Use a variety of techniques to sequence events so that they build on one another to create a coherent whole and build toward a particular tone and outcome (e.g., a sense of mystery, suspense, growth, or resolution).

CCSS.ELA-Literacy.W.11-12.5

Develop and strengthen writing as needed by planning, revising, editing, rewriting, or trying a new approach, focusing on addressing what is most significant for a specific purpose and audience. (Editing for conventions should demonstrate command of Language standards 1–3 up to and including grades 11–12 here.)

CCSS.ELA-Literacy.W.11-12.6

Use technology, including the Internet, to produce, publish, and update individual or shared writing products in response to ongoing feedback, including new arguments or information.

Research to Build and Present Knowledge:
CCSS.ELA-Literacy.W.11-12.7

Conduct short as well as more sustained research projects to answer a question (including a self-generated question) or solve a problem; narrow or broaden the inquiry when appropriate; synthesize multiple sources on the subject, demonstrating understanding of the subject under investigation.

CCSS.ELA-Literacy.W.11-12.8

Gather relevant information from multiple authoritative print and digital sources, using advanced searches effectively; assess the strengths and limitations of each source in terms of the task, purpose, and audience; integrate information into the text selectively to maintain the flow of ideas, avoiding plagiarism and overreliance on any one source and following a standard format for citation.

Listening:
CCSS.ELA-Literacy.SL.11-12.1.c

Propel conversations by posing and responding to questions that probe reasoning and evidence; ensure a hearing for a full range of positions on a topic or issue; clarify, verify, or challenge ideas and conclusions; and promote divergent and creative perspectives.

CCSS.ELA-Literacy.SL.11-12.1.d

Respond thoughtfully to diverse perspectives; synthesize comments, claims, and evidence made on all sides of an issue; resolve contradictions when possible; and determine what additional information or research is required to deepen the investigation or complete the task.

CCSS.ELA-Literacy.SL.11-12.2

Integrate multiple sources of information presented in diverse formats and media (e.g., visually, quantitatively, orally) in order to make informed decisions and solve problems, evaluating the credibility and accuracy of each source and noting any discrepancies among the data.

Presentation of Knowledge and Ideas:
CCSS.ELA-Literacy.SL.11-12.4

Present information, findings, and supporting evidence, conveying a clear and distinct perspective, such that listeners can follow the line of reasoning, alternative or opposing perspectives are addressed, and the organization, development, substance, and style are appropriate to purpose, audience, and a range of formal and informal tasks.[5]

Comment:

It is likely that most educated, intelligent adults would struggle to read these suggested texts in their entirety. Should Americans know these works? Yes. Every one of them? Perhaps not. Should we introduce them to students? Fine. Should we expect every student to know and be tested on their full understanding of all of them in all of their complexity, firing teachers whose students don't fare well on those tests?

After reading through just one area of the Common Core requirements for juniors and seniors, we should then take a look at the Common

Core mathematics requirements for elementary school children in first grade:

Operations and Algebraic Thinking in Grade 1:
[You read that correctly: "Algebraic Thinking in Grade 1.]
Determine the unknown whole number in an addition or subtraction equation relating three whole numbers. *For example, determine the unknown number that makes the equation true in each of the equations 8 + ? = 11, 5 = _ - 3, 6 + 6 = _.*

Add and subtract within 20, demonstrating fluency for addition and subtraction within 10. Use strategies such as counting on; making ten (e.g., 8 + 6 = 8 + 2 + 4 = 10 + 4 = 14); decomposing a number leading to a ten (e.g., 13 - 4 = 13 - 3 - 1 = 10 - 1 = 9); using the relationship between addition and subtraction (e.g., knowing that 8 + 4 = 12, one knows 12 - 8 = 4); and creating equivalent but easier or known sums (e.g., adding 6 + 7 by creating the known equivalent 6 + 6 + 1 = 12 + 1 = 13).

Compose two-dimensional shapes (rectangles, squares, trapezoids, triangles, half-circles, and quarter-circles) or three-dimensional shapes (cubes, right rectangular prisms, right circular cones, and right circular cylinders) to create a composite shape, and compose new shapes from the composite shape.

Partition circles and rectangles into two and four equal shares, describe the shares using the words *halves, fourths,* and *quarters,* and use the phrases *half of, fourth of,* and *quarter of.* Describe the whole as two of, or four of the shares. Understand for these examples that decomposing into more equal shares creates smaller shares.

Add within 100, including adding a two-digit number and a one-digit number, and adding a two-digit number and a multiple of 10, using concrete models or drawings and strategies based on place value, properties of operations, and/or the relationship between addition and subtraction; relate the strategy to a written method and explain the reasoning used. Understand that in adding two-digit numbers, one adds tens and tens, ones and ones; and sometimes it is necessary to compose a ten.

CCSS.Math.Content.1.NBT.C.5
Given a two-digit number, mentally find 10 more or 10 less than the number, without having to count; explain the reasoning used.[6]

Comment:
These statements were not goals but expectations that every first grader had to be able to do or the teacher was in trouble. Lofty goals are rightly expected, but curriculum that is written in the absence of classroom reality becomes a recipe for failures.

Rather than print out the entire Common Core, we should ask parents and members of the public who do not have children to access the Common Core online, to read it and become more familiar with it. Contrary to what some politicians claim, it is not without merit, but we should ask questions to make sure we understand what is being required of children, how quickly these curriculum changes and tests were made, and what was being demanded of children if they were to "succeed."

It might be prudent, as well, to ask about the origins of the Common Core. The Common Core State Standards Initiative can be traced to the State Educational Technology Directors Association (SETDA), the Partnership for the Assessment of Readiness for College and Careers (PARCC), and the Smarter Balanced Assessment Consortium (Smarter Balanced).[7] It is interesting to note that SETDA, by its own definition, is a technology-driven organization. Following ideas to their origins once again leads to interesting places.

NOTES

1. Every Student Succeeds Act (ESSA).
2. Ibid.
3. Common Core State Standards Initiative, Department of Defense Education Activity (DoDEA), (2015), www.corestandards.org.
4. Common Core State Standards.
5. Ibid.
6. Ibid.
7. Jones, R., and Fox, C. (2015). OER in Action: Implementation Highlights. Washington, D.C._SETDA, accessed October 20, 2015.

TEN
Why Students Should Read Tolstoy and Faulkner

We learn through telling stories. Narrative can play a significant role in other disciplines in terms of helping students engage with material. In his new book *A Beautiful Question*, Nobel Prize winning scientist Frank Wilczek wrote, "We humans are especially adapted to think in story and narrative to associate ideas with names and faces, and to find tales of conflicts . . . compelling."[1] If we use what "compels" us to pursue knowledge, we should, perhaps then, frame every academic endeavor in terms of narrative.

Wilczek incorporates Plato's totem of the cave as metaphor, as Plato did himself: "Plato thought big. He proposed a geometric theory of atoms and the universe . . . he was also a literary artist. His metaphor of the Cave [suggests] . . . the belief that everyday life offers us a mere shadow of reality . . . and that the essence is clearer and more beautiful than its shadow."[2]

Narratives allow us to learn, think, consider, frame in terms of story and identity, create context, imagine ourselves in or outside the frames of the stories, and conjecture. Novelist Norman Mailer wrote in the author's note to his novel about the CIA and Watergate: "[I]t is the author's contention that good fiction—if the writer can achieve it—is more real, that is more nourishing to our sense of reality, than nonfiction."[3]

Because Mailer was writing a work of fiction about a historical period in American history, his disclaimer is critical to understanding his purpose, but the author's notes as addendum to his fiction highlight an important reason that fiction may feel more real than nonfiction: "My hope is that the imagined world of *Harlot's Ghost* will bear more relation to the reality of these historical events than the spectrum of facts and often calculated misinformation that still surrounds them."[4] History should involve an analysis of "whose history" is being told; "facts" may be subjective, as well, if, as Mailer states, they are "calculated misinformation."

When we read "news" accounts of Putin's Russia that contain cultural and political biases, we know only the "enemy." If, however, we read Tolstoy, we know Russia and Russians as a people. They are no longer "the other" but fully realized human beings. This rings true of great literature. In addition to our visceral experience of otherness, literature allows us to witness, revisit, and experience existence in its nonlinear, chaotic state that often more closely resembles life than what we imagine through various other constructs.

In a recent lecture given in Syracuse, New York, renowned Shakespeare scholar Stephen Greenblatt stated, "As is so often with Shakespeare, the play [King Lear] opens with a conclusion and then completely unravels."[5] Greenblatt suggested that the mental process of believing we know the conclusion or answer and then being confronted with a chaotic unraveling of that conclusion more closely approximates our life experiences than our widely held assumptions about how the world is ordered.

Greenblatt drew on natural sciences, history, sociology, philosophy, biblical studies, and literature in his lecture "Age Is Unnecessary," an example of a powerful and deeply affective experience in which no single subject appeared in isolation. Near the completion of his talk, Greenblatt provided a quotation from the great Charles Darwin in speaking "to some larger truth." Darwin wrote in his autobiography:

> My mind seems to have become a kind of machine for grinding general laws out of large collections of facts, but why this should have caused the atrophy of that part of the brain alone, on which the higher tastes depend, I cannot conceive. A man with a mind more highly organized or better constituted than mine, would not, I suppose, have thus suffered; and if I had to live my life again, I would have made a rule to read some poetry and listen to some music at least once every week; for perhaps the parts of my brain now atrophied would thus have been kept active through use. The loss of these tastes is a loss of happiness, and may possibly be injurious to the intellect, and more probably to the moral character, by enfeebling the emotional part of our nature.[6]

Darwin, it would appear, understood the profundity of the loss when he turned from the arts. Here, the great and exacting scientist admits to a mistake in his approach: he did not make it a "rule to read some poetry and listen to some music at least once every week." Darwin would probably not have had much sympathy for the current STEM movement in education.

Reading literature is not easy nor is it hard fact. It is not designed to help us create the next generation of iPhone. Literature does not teach "lessons," as Vladimir Nabokov aptly put it, but it does connect us in ways that no other field of study is able to do so well. Nabokov wrote in his novel *Despair*, "To begin with, let us take the following motto . . . Literature is Love. Now we can continue."[7]

If you don't know the opening to Tolstoy's novel *Anna Karenina*, you should seek it out: "Happy families are all alike; every unhappy family is unhappy in its own way."[8] So begins Tolstoy's most perfect novel and one of the reasons why literature needs to be taught and read. Of course, reading *Anna Karenina* is not likely to lead to new technological developments nor will reading it affect the global economy.

Bluntly stated, reading *Anna Karenina* will not advance STEM education, ESSA, Race to the Top, No Child Left Behind, nor will it neatly meet the political agendas behind these twenty-first century "stakeholder" and data-driven mantras. Reading and writing about literature are not "how to" exercises; they are not, as some mistakenly assume, about encapsulating a message or moral of the story—that would be a fable. Rather than elaborate further in this listing of non-examples, I will point to the example of Tolstoy's words near the end of *Anna Karenina*:

> "Without knowing what I am and why I am here, life's impossible; and that I can't know, and so I can't live," Levin said to himself.
>
> "In infinite time, in infinite matter, in infinite space, is formed a bubble-organism, and that bubble lasts a while and bursts, and that bubble is Me."
>
> It was an agonizing error, but it was the sole logical result of ages of human thought in that direction.[9]

Tolstoy moves his characters through our most human dilemma: how to go on when we suffer:

> And Levin, a happy father and husband, in perfect health, was several times so near suicide that he hid the cord that he might not be tempted to hang himself, and was afraid to go out with his gun for fear of shooting himself.
>
> But Levin did not shoot himself, and did not hang himself; he went on living.[10]

Most of us do find a way to go on living. Reading and writing about literature is, of course, about acquiring new skills, too, learning close reading, analysis, thinking critically. But most importantly, literature is about life—everything beyond the classroom and our ability to control.

This becomes an argument about the very heart of education. Is the purpose of education only "career and college readiness?" Of course, reading and writing about *Anna Karenina* and other literature also fulfill that college and career readiness directive, just not in a neat linear formation. We are continually engaged in analyzing and synthesizing when we read challenging material, and those particular skills may be the most important ones we enhance through education.

A father of an interviewed teacher's former student stopped after an open house one evening and confronted her with a mild accusation.

"[Tim] loved your class, and he can't find a decent job! A lot of good all that English did him." The best part of this story, the teacher related, is that Tim found a great, well-paying job in a field he had not anticipated before going to college. It seems that a liberal arts degree teaches and encourages flexibility, and that is a quality that will be most valuable as young people enter an uncertain job market.

Not every classroom experience or class is a good one for a particular career or even for a particular student, although it may be perfect for someone else in the class. The fact we are not automatons makes lesson planning even more difficult; even the best examples of differentiated instruction will only go so far in meeting the needs of all of the students who are in unique situations.

A surprising fact about most teachers—that the public and politicians seem unaware of—is that they spend so many hours after "work" working. The following passage is from one interviewed teacher's journal. It is shown here to demonstrate reflective practice that takes place well beyond the boundaries of the "work day":

> Tonight, after recording my thoughts about the professional development workshop and grading a stack of student papers, I began reading an article in the October 23, 2006 issue of the *New Yorker* about Charles Darwin. It was a great read, not so much from a scientific point of view, but from an English educator's perspective. Darwin was as successful creating rhetoric as science, a major reason his science can be read today by educated people outside of the biological sciences.
>
> According to Gopnik, "Darwin was not a writer just by inclination; he was, uniquely among the great scientists, an author by trade." Adam Gopnik's article "Rewriting Nature: Charles Darwin, Natural Novelist" in the *Life and Letters* section of the magazine made me think about statements regarding what is a perceived lack of understanding of the importance of writing not just for clarity but for fluency and power. I think most teachers spend a great deal of time looking for new transitions, sources of information that will provide entry to material and discussion.
>
> What was particularly intriguing to me was the fact that Darwin's skills and abilities as a writer allowed him to make his case for evolution, according to Gopnik: "Darwin uses empirical instances not inductively, to build proof, but infectiously, to weaken resistance." Darwin's use of first person narrative, "copious detail," and artful speculation are what move the ideas behind *On the Origin of Species*.
>
> Gopnik notes, "Darwin's ability to look pious while demolishing every piety can be seen at its best in what may be the single most explosive sentence in English, which appears in the last chapter of *The Descent of Man*: 'We thus learn that man is descended from a hairy quadruped, furnished with a tail and pointed ears, probably arboreal in its habits, and an inhabitant of the Old World.'" If Darwin had framed that explosive sentence strictly as a scientist, how might it have looked or been interpreted? If he had couched it in scientific terms that con-

found non-science readers, perhaps evolution would not be so frightening to some people today nor would it be so well understood.[11]

Language and literature have enormous value beyond our understanding and appreciation of science, no matter how glorious that scientific discovery. In the preface to his best-selling text *Will in the World*, Stephen Greenblatt examines our endeavors in order "to understand how Shakespeare used his imagination to transform his life into his art" by reading and analyzing his literature.[12]

Laudable goals for a rich reading experience, but the second part of Greenblatt's statement is central to the advancement of everything we do: "it is important to use our own imagination."[13] To comprehend literature, to follow the ideas, study what led to the author's choices behind the diction, behind techniques, we must use analysis and our imaginations. When this happens, we have the potential to be become remarkable in any domain. Simply, and most profoundly, we have the opportunity to become remarkable as human beings.

Edward O. Wilson adds another dimension to this discussion about the importance of reading literature: "Within decades, knowledge within the technoscientific culture will of course be enormous compared to the present, but also the same everywhere in the world. What will continue to evolve and diversify indefinitely are the humanities. If our species can be said to have a soul, it lives in the humanities."[14]

Wilson articulates the importance of science, but he makes a compelling argument for redefining our STEM definitions to become more inclusive of the arts. Without all of our voices, our literature, our language, our art, our music, we are floating in a sea of indifference and into a technologically perfect, hollow architecture.

NOTES

1. Wilczek, *A Beautiful Question*, 4.
2. Ibid, 4–5.
3. Norman Mailer, Author's Note, *Harlot's Ghost* (New York: Random House, 2007), 1287–88.
4. Mailer, *Harlot's Ghost*, 1288.
5. Stephen Greenblatt, "Age Is Unnecessary" (lecture).
6. Ibid.
7. Vladimir Nabokov, *Despair* (New York: Vantage International Ed., Division of Random House, 1989), 117.
8. Leo Tolstoy, *Anna Karenina*, 1.
9. Tolstoy, *Anna Karenina*, 840.
10. Ibid.
11. Interviewed teacher's journal (Interview on December 7, 2014).
12. Greenblatt, *Will in the World: How Shakespeare Became Shakespeare* (New York: W. W. Norton and Co., 2004), 14.
13. Greenblatt, *Will in the World*.
14. Wilson, *The Meaning of Human Existence*, 185.

ELEVEN
Consequences of Exclusionary Parameters

According to the Office of Innovation and Improvement (OII), the STEM (science, technology, engineering, and math) Team at the US Department of Education, STEM is the answer to an "ever-changing, increasingly complex world; it's more important than ever that our nation's youth are prepared to bring knowledge and skills to solve problems, make sense of information, and know how to gather and evaluate evidence to make decisions; these are the kinds of skills that students develop in science, technology, engineering and math—disciplines collectively known as STEM."[1]

What a surprise to find that students only develop the skills to "make sense of information" in STEM subjects. This team, made up of government and private corporation executives who lead OII has determined that the skills of "how to gather and evaluate evidence to make decisions" can best be learned not through language, history, art, foreign language, or any other humanities courses but in STEM courses. How the determination that flies in the face of logic is made seems unimportant to the STEM–rolling express train.

STEM is also, most importantly, tied to school funding: "Because of the government and business funding initiatives, becoming a STEM-designated school can mean access to significant financial resources."[2] Unfortunately, school administrators cannot afford to consider other options if they want their districts to share in that funding stream.

Although, as previously stated, the definitions of what a STEM school consists of vary, New York State Education Department provides parameters quite clearly:

1. STEM FOR ALL: All students must attain STEM literacy for the Empire State to thrive in the 21st century
2. SYSTEMIC MODEL: A systemic, interdisciplinary approach to STEM teaching and learning is required to prepare the "whole" student for success in work and life
3. EVIDENCE-BASED APPROACH: Effective STEM education must leverage existing assets and embrace new models that reflect real world context, interests and needs of students, teachers, and their communities
4. OPEN COLLABORATIVE INNOVATION: Innovative STEM education policies, processes and programs must be both scalable and sustainable
5. COMMITTED STAKEHOLDERS: Business, PK–20 education, students, parents, community organizations, foundations and government must engage steadfastly, openly, and with ingenuity across a broad spectrum of interests, expertise and capacities to achieve STEM excellence.[3]

STEM—science, technology, engineering, mathematics. Nearly every discussion of the STEM movement makes a disclaimer that the "arts" (lumping together English, history, art, music, foreign language, social policy, economics, public affairs, physical education, and everything else) are important, too, as long as they are used to somehow support technology and engineering education. Perception becomes the reality.

Considering counterclaims of STEM proponents—STEM is inclusive, as demonstrated in the phrase, "interdisciplinary approach to STEM teaching and learning," intending that the humanities are included in that caveat "interdisciplinary approach."

The reality experienced by millions involved in STEM education, as policymakers discuss and direct it, in actuality, only relates to applied career fields in technology and engineering. There is very little discussion of theoretical sciences and mathematics outside of the practical application of engineering and problem solving in technology. There is too little discourse on evolution as a central tenant of human biology and development. There is no discussion of physics in which the origins of the universe are considered. Even if we foolishly agree to chop off every other discipline, there is something missing.

In other words, the STEM acronym in education should really be called TE, representing just the teaching of technology and engineering. The acronym is not only tremendously exclusionary but harmful and misleading. Scientists who understand the implications of STEM in public education should be as concerned as teachers of the humanities that STEM, as it has been rolled out, has taken such a firm hold in America.

Projecting what these multitudes of STEM graduates will do in a few years, John Cassidy in his article "College Calculus: What's the Real Value of Higher Education" should give us pause to stop and consider just where we think we are going with STEM education. Cassidy examines Wharton professor Peter Cappelli's view of exactly where it is our STEM graduates-in-the-making are going: "Cappelli reports that only about a fifth of recent graduates with STEM degrees got jobs that made use of that training. 'The evidence for recent grads suggests clearly that there is no overall shortage of STEM grads.'"[4]

Cassidy notes in the *New Yorker* that Cappelli frames an argument that is not about the failure of STEM but the advantages of the liberal arts:

> "To be clear, the idea is not that there will be a big financial payoff to a liberal arts degree," Cappelli writes. "It is that there is no guarantee of a payoff from very practical, work-based degrees either, yet that is all those degrees promise. For liberal arts, the claim is different and seems more accurate, that it will enrich your life and provide lessons that extend beyond any individual job. There are centuries of experience providing support for that notion."[5]

The idea our lives may become richer and deeper through our exposure to art and literature should have inherent value and not be discarded for some notion of expediency. It is likely that expediency, however, is not the issue. Rather, the turning away from the humanities has deep political overtones.

We might want to consider the genesis of this "reform" movement and who will profit from the "mass production" of engineers? It might also be crucial to examine what happens to those American educated engineers who are laid off or fired when the company finds cheaper engineers in India, Pakistan, or some other area of the world.

Even if we consider the broadest possible definition of engineer, we are still limiting scholars, attacking problem solving from the trench rather than the far-away mountain as the mathematician John Nash did.[6] The discussion surrounding STEM involves the number of engineering jobs that students must be "career ready" for after schooling.

In his article in the *Atlantic* on the future of work in the United States, Derek Thompson asks us to consider this new world not as very far off from the one we are living in currently:

> And when they [economists and technologists] look up from their spreadsheets, they see automation high and low—robots in the operating room and behind the fast-food counters. They imagine self-driving cars snaking through the streets and Amazon drones dotting the sky, replacing millions of drivers, warehouse stockers, and retail workers. They observe the capabilities of machines—already formidable—continue to expand exponentially, while our own remain the same. And they wonder: Is any job truly safe?[7]

Thompson and others who have considered a technology-driven future recognize that today's occupations are unlikely to exist in a few years.

Which brings us to the question of how do we educate young people for this kind of uncertainty? Should "college and career readiness" be based on teaching for technology jobs currently in existence?

Should we, rather, help young people think for themselves, read critically and know history and context, write analytically and well, study diverse subjects that bolster imagination, the psyche, and soul. Teach them skills in order to guide them in becoming flexible in their expectations and career searches. Teach them to be creative and innovative by approaching problems from diverse points of view. Teach them to value others and understand the world beyond their borders.

IS STEM EDUCATION NECESSARY FOR INNOVATION?

As previously noted, educating people for narrowly defined careers is not a smart, long-term strategy in public education. Examining a particular application of STEM in Florida, Drs. Lynne Holt, David Colburn, and Lynn Leverty wrote up their findings after performing research conducted at the University of Florida and stated:

> STEM occupations accounted for only 6% of total occupations in the U.S. in May 2009. By 2018, STEM jobs are projected to increase in both Florida and the nation but are not projected to exceed 4% of total jobs in Florida. So a cogent argument can be made for focusing less on occupations and more on the attributes of a STEM education that benefit the entire population and speak more broadly to workforce needs.[8]

The Bureau of Economic and Business Research team of Holt, Colburn, and Leverty recommends STEM education as helpful in creating situations in which innovation may occur with a caveat: "STEM education is arguably important not as an end in itself, but is a means of making people innovative and productive in all their endeavors."[9]

However, educators are fully aware that there is no formula for what "makes people innovative and productive in all their endeavors." How exactly does a STEM education make people innovative? It is more than likely that there are multiple paths to innovation and productivity, or we would not still be in existence as a species and definitely would not have made the achievements we have accomplished.

The political and business-driven push for STEM arose out of the supposed "crisis" in education, yet there is ample evidence that this is largely a hyperbolic claim. According to Robert N. Charette, in his article, "The STEM Crisis Is a Myth," this crisis had been predicted again and again since the 1930s.[10]

Charette also noted in his article in *IEEE Spectrum*:

> [A]longside such dire projections, you'll also find reports suggesting just the opposite—that there are more STEM workers than suitable

jobs. One study found, for example, that wages for U.S. workers in computer and math fields have largely stagnated since 2000. Even as the Great Recession slowly recedes, STEM workers at every stage of the career pipeline, from freshly minted grads to mid- and late-career Ph.D.'s, still struggle to find employment as many companies, including Boeing, IBM, and Symantec, continue to lay off thousands of STEM workers.[11]

The reality of business needs for engineers has a shelf life that we do not know the end dates on yet, but educating everyone for engineering careers is not only impractical but unwise. Why would this illogical charge from business interests be allowed to dominate education policy at every level? Charette makes some of the same claims that are made in this text—politics and powerful business interests dominate:

> Clearly, powerful forces must be at work to perpetuate the cycle. One is obvious: the bottom line. Companies would rather not pay STEM professionals high salaries with lavish benefits, offer them training on the job, or guarantee them decades of stable employment. So having an oversupply of workers, whether domestically educated or imported, is to their benefit. It gives employers a larger pool from which they can pick the "best and the brightest," and it helps keep wages in check. No less an authority than Alan Greenspan, former chairman of the Federal Reserve, said as much when in 2007 he advocated boosting the number of skilled immigrants entering the United States so as to "suppress" the wages of their U.S. counterparts, which he considered too high.[12]

What happens when business interests do not dominate education? Physicist Frank Wilczek asks the question, "Does the world embody beautiful ideas?' in his book *A Beautiful Question: Finding Nature's Deep Design.*"[13] His seemingly simple question leads to the formulation of a multitude of other questions and a journey that takes readers from the pre-quantum physics of Plato and Pythagoras to the discovery of the Higgs particle in a treatise that is as beautifully written as the concepts he explores. Wilczek discusses the fact that his own scientific discoveries arose out of questions involving interest in the concept of symmetry that he, initially, found in art and language.

Within Wilczek's text is a representation of the convergence of science, mathematics, art, history, and the English language. It is quite simply a blueprint for what education could be.

STEM—science, technology, engineering, mathematics. Nearly every discussion of the STEM education reform movement in the United States makes some type of disclaimer that the acronym is meant to include other disciplines, but how these disciplines figure into the equations are imprecisely defined, if at all. It is not enough to add an "A" to STEM to include the "arts" because the term "arts" is far too broad, even inaccurate, as a representation of all other fields of study.

STEM education—as it is typically discussed by policymakers, not other educators—substantially relates to applied career fields in technology and engineering. There is very little conversation on theoretical sciences or pure mathematics outside of the applications to problem solving in engineering and technology. In other words, the STEM movement that was meant to excite students and educators about mathematics, the sciences, technology, and engineering may have an unintended effect: one that feels exclusionary—even demeaning—in substantive discourse and implementation.

Education reform is too vitally important to exclude other educators or large segments of student scholars in the conversation. We need everyone at the table if we want to make meaningful progress.

Understanding the impetus behind the STEM acronym and the subsequent movement is central to considerations of how we continue to define our American public and private school offerings. STEM arose largely out of manufacturing and industry needs for qualified engineering candidates for newly created jobs. Part of the reason these jobs were not being filled had to do with the inability to predict the exploding growth of the technology industry. If we too narrowly define this next wave of education reform, we face the likelihood of making the same miscalculation again because of the difficulty of predicting the future.

Reform, therefore, must reflect a journey that moves well beyond filling "a dearth of engineering slots." Who can predict the available jobs eighteen years from today? We certainly could not do this eighteen years ago, or eighteen years before that with a great deal of accuracy. Tomorrow's jobs are likely to look vastly different from those available today.

Yet there are skill sets everyone needs in a constantly changing global market, as well as skills people need in order to do more than simply survive. Those skill sets include some that have been previously identified and included in the STEM focus, critical thinking and problem solving, as well as some that have been identified but not yet taken center stage with problem solving, formulating the right questions, reading and writing any and all materials analytically, and considering ideas from multiple perspectives in order to approach innovation.

Further, what transpires when a young engineer discovers that he or she hates his or her job? What happens when he is miserable in the day-to-day details of what this occupation entails? One powerful antidote is suggested in a lecture given in Syracuse, New York, in October 2015 by noted author and Shakespeare scholar Stephen Greenblatt. Professor Greenblatt related an anecdote about his own career path that led him to a bridge in England, where he stood with a document in his hand—the awaited letter of acceptance to a prestigious law school.

Greenblatt told the audience that he tore up that acceptance letter and let the pieces be carried away because he had made a discovery about himself and what he wanted to do with his life.[14] What becomes of our young engineers—the ones we have prolifically turned out of our STEM schools—when they suddenly decide to tear up this contract?

Education should not be about predetermining futures of young people or fitting them into career positions that may not even exist when they graduate. We need to help students discover their passions—yes, passions—because interest is what drives scholarship and success in every discipline, as well as builds a sense of identity and ethics. Even if we consider the broadest possible definition of the term "engineer," we are still limiting scholars, attacking problem solving from the trenches rather than the far-away mountain.

Symposiums and policymaking around STEM take for granted the number of engineering jobs that students must be career ready for after schooling. Not surprisingly, there is very little discourse on the topic of what these engineers will do when potential employers turn down qualified young people because they can find someone in another country who will work for less. Business decisions are based in economics. If there is a way to make a greater profit, business will move to this model regardless of the number of jobs created or eliminated.

Regarding the STEM "solution," Laurence A. Moran, professor in the Department of Biochemistry at the University of Toronto, wrote in his blog:

> "Science" is NOT the same as "technology" and not the same as "engineering." There's a big difference between learning science and learning how to build things. The purpose of a degree in technology and engineering is obvious—it's job training. The purpose of a science education is quite different—it's supposed to teach you how to think critically.[15]

In "The Problem with STEM" that appears in Moran's blog "Sandwalk: Strolling with a Skeptical Biochemist," he emphasizes the idea that the goal of science education, "should be no different than the educational goals in history, philosophy, or English literature. It's to teach students how to think."[16]

Blending of supposedly vastly different fields of study is routine for serious scholars, but for a variety of reasons, this kind of thinking is also something we shy away from in educating students until they reach the highest levels. Stephen Greenblatt said, "There is no break between what history is and what science is,"[17] referring to the concept that deep knowledge crosses these artificial barriers we have constructed.

Although the concept appears radical in the current climate of education reform, it is an idea that is shared by some of the best in their fields of study, including Edward O. Wilson, who wrote in *The Meaning of Human Existence*, "The most successful scientist thinks like a poet—wide-ranging, sometimes fantastical—and works like a bookkeeper."[18]

If we adopt this more complex approach, children will learn, but it will be difficult because it involves things like flexibility in structures and procedures in how schools are set up. There are universal skills that can be taught across all discipline, however, such as analysis and synthesis, and framing and postulating questions.

We should be educating children to learn to read with skepticism across disciplines, explore areas deeply and with sustained focus—even passion—to reach for what they do not know about themselves and the world in every course of study. We have an opportunity to focus on teaching skills that human beings need to create science or narrative, mathematics or art, to become innovators in any field, to tackle difficult problems that arise in every human endeavor.

Educating children must be about more than college and career readiness for jobs that exist in the year 2015. Educating children should be about more than technological expansion. When we look to human history, we make discoveries about our present and are able to better envision our futures.

NOTES

1. OII, http://innovation.ed.gov/what-we-do/stem/.
2. STEMSchool.com, http://www.stemschool.com/articles/what-is-stem-education/
3. New York State Education STEM.
4. John Cassidy, "College Calculus: What's the Real Value of Higher Education?" *New Yorker* (September 7, 2015), accessed September 1, 2015, http://www.newyorker.com/magazine/2015/09/07/college-calculus.
5. Cassidy, "College Calculus."
6. Ted Sherman and Myles Ma, "Famed 'A Beautiful Mind', Mathematician John Nash, Wife, Killed in N.J. Turnpike Crash," *NJ Advance Media* for NJ.com (May 28, 2015), accessed October 2, 2015, http://www.nj.com/middlesex/index.ssf/2015/05/famed_a_beautiful_mind_mathematician_wife_killed_in_taxi_crash_police_say.html.
7. Thompson, "A World Without Work," 52.
8. David Colburn, et. al., "Innovation and STEM Education," Reubin O. D. Askew Institute on Politics and Society, BEHR, University of Florida (2015), accessed October 10, 2015, https://www.bebr.ufl.edu/content/innovation-and-stem-education.
9. Colburn et al. "Innovation and STEM Education."
10. Robert N. Charette, "The STEM Crisis Is a Myth," *IEEE Spectrum* (August 30, 2013), accessed October 20, 2015, http://spectrum.ieee.org/at-work/education/the-stem-crisis-is-a-myth.
11. Ibid.
12. Ibid.
13. Wilczek, *Beautiful Question*, 4.
14. Greenblatt, lecture.
15. Laurence A. Moran, "The Problem with STEM," *Sandwalk: Strolling with a Skeptical Biochemist* (November 11, 2011), accessed October 27, 2015, http://sandwalk.blogspot.com/2011/11/problem-with-stem.html.
16. Moran, "The Problem with STEM."
17. Greenblatt, lecture.
18. Wilson, 41.

TWELVE
Education without the Humanities

All around us are harbingers of doom, the coming apocalypse, zombies, and the not-so-thinly vailed racism behind the zombie craze and fears. Since we are surrounded by predictions of doom, I'd like to offer another story that allows us to speculate on the consequences of our actions if we follow the policies, legislation recently passed, and plans proposed to the letter.

It is easy for America to cheer on the racist and clueless comments about excising hard-working and dedicated teachers and teachers' unions and starting up "glorious" charter schools. Just look at the editorializing we find in the *Chicago Tribune* by contact reporter Kristen McQueary, in an editorial entitled "Chicago, New Orleans, and Rebirth," in which she praises the effects of New Orleans's tragedy: "Hurricane Katrina gave a great American city a rebirth."[1] Looking to wipe away Chicago's teachers and unions with the wrath and destructive force of a hurricane, McQueary states:

> Envy isn't a rational response to the upcoming 10-year anniversary of Hurricane Katrina. But with Aug. 29 fast approaching and New Orleans Mayor Mitch Landrieu making media rounds, including at the *Tribune* Editorial Board, I find myself wishing for a storm in Chicago — an unpredictable, haughty, devastating swirl of fury. A dramatic levee break. Geysers bursting through manhole covers. A sleeping city, forced onto the rooftops.[2]

Editorializing, politicizing, McQueary shows evidence of racism in an editorial that should give everyone pause about hitting the "reset button" on public schools. The story, by the book's author, that follows asks us to consider what our future might look like if we continue with this imbalanced position of STEM schools and deconstructing public education for charter schools.

Chapter 12
RISE OF TECH-COS

Even though it only happens once or twice a year, every Friday the 13th, a group of us—my best friends in the whole world—commit some act of sabotage in order to make ourselves feel like we are protesting the formation of COS and its unholy alliance with TEch. Dad says he still secretly mourns the end of the United States of America. I only share this information with four people, but when we stand and recite the TEch-Confederacy of States (COS) pledge each morning, I'm actually silently mouthing the words to my favorite song.

I mention silently because, even though I'm brave and all, I may not have stated the fact that someone gets shot and killed every couple of weeks at our school. Dad says that is pretty bad even in comparison to the old days when kids would walk into school with a gun periodically. Now, with everyone openly carrying a semi-automatic, you never know who is going to go off or for what.

Last week, my English teacher was killed because he brought up Shakespeare again, at least that's what Caleb said when he opened fire. Mr. Wright never even had a chance to pull his own gun from his waist band. The worst part is, I liked Mr. Wright and Shakespeare, but even I know that Mr. Wright wasn't supposed to be talking about Shakespeare with us. We've got a TEch-COS English curriculum that includes reading manuals for complicated parts and systems, followed by Bible recitations. All of us are slated to be TEchy engineers someday because we're pretty good at math. I'm pretty good at writing, too, but writing manuals every day gets kind of boring.

"Never want to hear that name Shakespeare again," said Caleb before walking out. His rich parents claimed self-defense and the fact that Mr. Wright was threatening by his very nature and his anti-TEchy-COS leanings. They also suspected he was trying to create a war on Christianity. After citing our state's "Stand Your Ground" law, Caleb was back in school by the end of the first semester. He pretty much gets to do whatever he wants in every class because all of the teachers are afraid of him and afraid of our parents and the administration that works for TEch.

To be honest, I don't ever remember Mr. Wright threatening anyone except to say that if we refused to question, read, and write, we would continue to dumb down an already mind-numbingly dysfunctional and impoverished society of prisoner, automatons, and yes men. I wasn't sure what a yes man was, but I never asked him because we don't really ask questions in school. Mr. Wright should have known that.

"He just liked to push writing 'cause his name was Wright," said Caleb, who owns six automatic weapons, two antique handguns from his grandfather, and a one Redneck Toothpick knife he likes to call his *baby* that he brought in for show and tell the first week of third grade. He still carries it every day, three years later. Mr. Wright is the fourth person

Caleb has killed; the first three were kids that didn't go to school. Somehow they counted less, I guess because nothing happened to him then either. His father is one of the higher ups in TEch in our state.

Dad says that he wishes he could take me out of this school, and it's costing him, "an arm and a leg," but there are no other options except a couple of online schools that have been proven to be fraudulent or are already going bankrupt. Dad likes to tell me about the old days when every kid could attend a public school for free, there was a federal government and laws to protect individual rights, including freedom of religion, as well as separation of church and state. I just laugh.

Only a few of the kids I knew growing up actually go to school. Most of the rest work for the State Work Reward (SWR) program you can get into as early as six years old now. They just kind of disappear once they go in. A few of my former friends and neighbors are now in the prison system, the largest in the world, we state with pride as part of the TEch-COS pledge.

Dad told me that there used to be child labor and other laws created to protect children that would have prevented this, but I think some kids are just as glad to be in the work program or in prison rather than in a home where they have nothing to eat. To be honest, the day after Mr. Wright was shot, I thought about quitting and joining the SWR, too. Dad would have been pretty upset with me, though, so I'm trying to finish up here.

Dad's still a believer in engineering, even though his engineering job was outsourced to India. No matter how little you earn, Dad says, there is always someone, somewhere willing to work for less. Fortunately, Dad was able to continue to work by writing the manuals for TEch. That's why he tells me to pay attention in English.

TEch supremacy and the Confederacy of States (COS) were inevitable, according to Dad, once the anti-government types took over. Funny thing, Dad says, "We have far more restrictions and fewer freedoms now." My dad tells me he remembers the day he first knew it was coming when I was still too little to remember.

"I was standing in a long line at the Verizon store for my new iPhone—okay, I'll explain what that is later, but let's just say they were a lot like our handhelds today—when this young man walked up to the front of the line and said to the salesman, 'I'm here to fix my phone, if you people can fix it, because I know you're all in league with the government and not that I'm paranoid or anything, but you probably have my every move monitored. The government needs to be taken down.'

"The poor sales clerk never even blinked but told the guy that he'd be happy to help and understood his frustration, which was a very good thing because the next comment out of the dude's mouth was that he was carrying, not as a threat, of course, he said, but it was a threat, and I was suddenly glad that there were half a dozen people between us."

"Nobody between us anymore," I say.

Dad nods, lowering his head, and then touching the top of mine as if he is going to ruffle my hair, but he doesn't. He tells me he is still surprised at how quickly our democracy crumbled, our public schools disappeared, our rights and freedoms swallowed up, and a few corporations dictated all of daily life.

My school—TEch102—is owned and operated by TEch Corp., a global corporation that operates about one-half of the schools in our state and around COS. The others are owned by Animatronics Inc. There is one Animatronics school about seventy miles away, but it's not too practical to try to get there and back every day, Dad says. He doesn't think things would be any better at Animatronics102 either. They have the same COS-dictated curriculum.

The old days of history, art, music, and literature are long gone, he says sadly. I remind him that we still have a history about the rise of COS and TEch, "the greatest entities the world has ever known."

After TEch and Animatronics Inc., there is All Energy Corp. and Incarceration Corp., the largest employers in our state and other states in COS. Dad told me that most of his old friends are in the Incarceration Corp.'s prison system, now, making tech products for the rest of us. When I asked him how they got there, he just shakes his head and says, "asking too many questions."

"Never forget, we are subservient to TEch," Dad says, rubbing the top of my head, as if negating his words.

Sometimes late at night, Dad will sneak a book out from underneath our floorboards and read to me. I love the sound of his voice even though I don't understand most of the words. Then he tells me wonderful stories about the days when there were these mysterious places like libraries and colleges for anyone who could take out a loan. There was elementary and secondary education available free of charge for all Americans.

"Sounds like more fairy tales," I say, when he kisses me goodnight, getting up to leave.

"I miss the old days badly," Dad says suddenly, as he sits back down at the foot of my twin bed.

"I miss Mom," I add; then we remain in silence, passively looking at our handhelds.

NOTES

1. Kristen McQueary, "Chicago, New Orleans, and Rebirth," *Chicago Tribune* (August 13, 2015), accessed November 1, 2015, http://www.chicagotribune.com/news/opinion/commentary/ct-chicago-katrina-financial-disaster-landrieu-new-orleans-mcqueary-emanuel-pers-20150813-column.html.

2. McQueary, "Chicago, New Orleans, and Rebirth."

THIRTEEN
What You Don't Know

What we do not know, what we fail to consider, can and will hurt us. One idea fostered by many politicians and business people, who are interested in increasing their fortunes via the education market, is that teachers are lazy and need to be fired, but the myth is not supported by the reality. Teachers, for the greatest part, go into a profession in which they are comparatively poorly compensated for their years of schooling and expertise. Why? They want to help children.

If mistakes are made by teachers in a classroom, the problem often has more to do with policy, teacher training, school management, and school funding than teacher intent or practice. Sustaining myths about teachers and teaching is dangerous for a number of reasons, but the most important being that we will be unable to address the very real issues that need to be resolved if we focus on the wrong targets.

While there are, undoubtedly, teachers who are not very good at their jobs, just as there are professionals and trade people in every walk of life who are not particularly good at what they do, nearly every teacher can improve in their delivery and content with coordinated, well-grounded in pedagogy, professional development that is delivered in a fashion that allows for growth and is not contradictory or punitive in implementation.

Here again, problems in instructional delivery can be addressed within a system that is already in place if the administration is aware of the context and content of the professional development that has previously taken place, as well as how it is aligned to the current offering. Administration can also assign excellent and experienced teachers to mentor teachers who are struggling in their educational delivery. While mentoring programs exist for new teachers and for teachers on "tip plans" or in danger of being fired, these programs could be in place to help any teacher at any point in his or her career. Remove the threat, and people tend to respond positively.

Another harmful artifice in education reform involves the push for the establishment of new charter schools and local control. This movement—away from free, public schools and toward privatization—will leave many students out of the picture. Local control is also largely a fallacy in that many of those pushing for charter schools are financially involved across states and boundaries, influencing decisions in order to make profits in the charter school industry. In other words, it is not about the children or improving their opportunities.

In Douglas County, Colorado, Brian Malone put the "dots together" and recognized what was behind the education "reform" not only in his district but in other areas of the country. He risked his career; well, he risked everything, to get at the truth and made a powerful film entitled *Education, Inc.* because what the people in his district and across the country did not know could very well hurt them.

Douglas County is located mid-way between Denver and Colorado Springs. Using just one school district, Malone's film makes clear what is behind the "reform" taking place across the country, and it is not about children or school reform at all. Quoting, with permission, from the master script of his film:

> On the other sides of this election [for local school board members], a handful of some very wealthy people and their organizations have spent a lot of money to keep these local citizens from running their own school district. In fact, they've outspent these citizens about ten to one. In all, more than a million dollars has been spent on this local school board election. . . . The majority of that million dollars has come from a small handful of billionaires and millionaires outside of Douglas County, like Jeb Bush, The Koch Brothers, Michael Bloomberg, the billionaire who founded JD Edwards, an oil and gas magnate . . . and a commercial real estate developer. These guys don't live here . . . and they don't have kids in our public schools. So why are they pouring all of this money into a local school board election?
>
> William Bennett, the former Secretary of Education under Ronald Reagan, was also added to the district's roster for paid opinions. Bennett wrote and published his own paper, supporting the district and its reforms. He followed up with a live appearance and a speech in Douglas County, just before the election. Both his paper and his appearance were paid for by the district's non-profit arm.[1] It is fairly safe to state that many Americans are entirely unaware of this approach by millionaires involved in school board elections in states other than those in which the millionaires reside. School board elections are something typically within the purview of local communities. The complexity of the "approach" makes it difficult to understand without considerable research, for the reason that many Americans do not connect the dots

to charter school openings and the line to profits. The costs of closing public schools are far greater than empirical data alone will provide.

The idea that education is in "local control" appears to be a relic of the past, with big money interests invested all over the country, changing outcomes, unless we make the collective decision to return the authority to create change with educators not politicians.

The issue here is not about a particular candidate, but candidates for high public office who have created platforms and policy ideology that continue to dominate the cultural and political landscape long after they have vacated the scene.

What language or terminology has dominated the political scene and the cultural landscape? Our discussions now start with acceptance of charter schools as alternatives. There is ample evidence from multiple, reliable sources that student performance, or student outcome, in charter schools is no better, and often much worse, than those compared to students' outcomes in public school settings. Charter schools are not a solution or panacea.

The state of Louisiana has one of the worst student performance records, despite the fact that Louisiana moved almost exclusively to the charter school model.[2] If we examine the facts first before moving toward policy directives, we will be less likely to make egregious errors that affect millions of children across the country.

Considering the rhetorical fallacy of statistics from small numbers, *Washington Post* reporter Valerie Strauss points out the obvious problems found in a former governor's promotion of charter schools all over the country, based on his tenure in Florida:

> What he didn't mention was a big charter school study last year that concluded that Florida charter schools had math and reading test scores that were either no better or worse than traditional public schools. And he didn't note that a disproportionate number of charters get failing academic letter grades from the state (an accountability measure that Bush pioneered). Nor did he note that the charter scene in Florida has been marred in the past decade by numerous closures of charters—some even during the school year—and a number of scandals about financial mismanagement. Among all the states, Florida, incidentally, has the second-highest number of for-profit charter schools.[3]

Strauss also addresses here a seldom discussed feature of charter schools: their failure to offer education to all students. It is one thing to boast high test scores, but if the only students accepted into the school are high-achieving students, then any comparison with public schools should be null and void: "Charter schools in general don't educate the same number of English Language Learners and students with severe disabilities as traditional schools, making many comparisons unfair."[4]

As the evidence is examined, conclusions based on small numbers become even more damning. Yet finding the information about the discrepancies between what these charter school proponents claim and the facts are actually difficult to find in mainstream media. Where do we find public discourse concerning the children that charter schools reject?

These are not questions that easily find their way into television coverage of the policy debate. This lack of attention to the important particulars in platforms is particularly disturbing. There is a relationship to what we say in public life and how that changes the cultural dialectic.

The focus here is not on any one elected official or candidate for higher office, but on a political process that, too often, finds our leaders and would-be leaders creating policy or advocating for policies that are compromised from the start. Conflicts of interest have been around nearly as long as we have been a country, but for education "reform" to be possible and not a sound bite, we need different players in the equations.

Kinder in her assessment of political education reformers and their intentions, Dana Goldstein wrote in her book *The Teacher Wars: A History of America's Most Embattled Profession*, "[E]ducation reformers today should learn from the mistakes of history."[5] Even a barely passing knowledge of education history shows ample evidence that what is being lauded as new reform has already been tried and been shown to be ineffective if not damaging.

Dismantling public schools and setting up "competing" private schools with public funds by private investors is a very big business, and it is also a form of stealing not only public funds but public trust and our future.

NOTES

1. Brian Malone, *Education, Inc. For Profit. For Kids?*
2. Singer, "Despite Big Problems Charters Attract Hedge Fund Support."
3. Strauss, "Jeb Bush Bashes Traditional Public Schools."
4. Ibid.
5. Goldstein, *Teacher Wars*, 11.

FOURTEEN
Master Teachers in Every Classroom

How do gluons bind matter? Or for that matter (pun intended), what are gluons? The broader question is how do we get kids interested and invested in, even passionate about, science and mathematics? This is not a question related to which courses should be cut to promote science and mathematics in schools. It should not be a question of firing some teachers while giving bonuses to others.

While the intentions of creating a master teacher, a more lucrative program for teachers of science and mathematics, is designed to help teachers focus on improving student performance in these critical fields, the effect in a school may be more damaging than the educational practices currently in place. Between intent and effect there is a vast expanse of area where different results are likely.

In September 2014, US Secretary of Education Arne Duncan announced, "the award of $35 million for 24 new partnerships between universities and high-need school districts that will recruit, train and support more than 11,000 teachers over the next five years—primarily in science, technology, engineering and math (STEM) fields—to improve student achievement."[1]

At the state and federal levels, additional money and prestige are being attached to teachers in science, technology, engineering, and math fields only. Perception is reality. Considering counterclaims that STEM is inclusive and intends to bring the humanities into the reform movement through supporting STEM subjects, the allocation of funds alone is enough to be divisive and reveal a bias that reflects business interests more than student interests.

When the Supreme Court struck down part of the Voting Rights Act of 1965 in June 2013, with the ruling that in effect stated we are "living in a post-racial era," the reality was again altered negatively for millions of

Americans. Chief Justice Roberts stated, "Congress did not use the record it compiled to shape a coverage formula grounded in current conditions. It instead reenacted a formula based on 40-year-old facts having no logical relation to the present day."[2]

Racial prejudice evidenced forty years ago is still very much in evidence today, as any number of Americans will attest to and counter Chief Justice Roberts's claim. The "Black Lives Matter" movement arising in 2015 is direct evidence that black Americans do not feel Chief Justice Roberts's sense of post-racial. Feeling like second class citizens within your own country is a daily insult.

Students and teachers who are not within the STEM purview feel another type of insult—a less-than status. Imagine that in whatever you do for a living, you have just been told that four specific people you work with are eligible for promotions, but only those four because they have blonde hair and blue eyes. It is irrelevant that you have been at your job longer, are far more proficient at it than the four selected, and your results are far better than those of the four blondes.

There is a rationale for this decision by the powers that be, however. They would like to see more blondes apply for jobs at your place of work. Makes sense, doesn't it? No?

In New York State, Governor Cuomo and the State Education Department decreed that STEM teachers were eligible to receive $15,000 stipends annually over a four-year period. That is an additional $60,000 that teachers in the humanities were not eligible to receive. How does a teacher apply to become a master teacher? In New York State, the eligibility requirements are spelled out on the New York State Master Teacher website:

> To be eligible for the New York State Master Teacher program, you must:
>
> - Be a certified, currently employed teacher in New York State, with a minimum of 4 years of experience teaching STEM disciplines.
> - Have a current course load of at least 60% in STEM disciplines, teaching grades 6–12 and plans to maintain the 60% STEM course load.
> - Be rated "effective" or "highly effective" on your Annual Professional Performance Review.[3]

If you are a teacher in any discipline other than mathematics and science, you are NOT eligible to apply for the Master Teacher program, status, or pay.

New York State governor, Andrew Cuomo, is quoted on this website as stating:

> We want the best possible teachers in every New York classroom educating our children. As part of the state's work to transform our educa-

tion system and put students first, we are committed to investing in great teachers to educate our students and create a highly-trained workforce to drive our future economy. This program will reward those teachers who work harder to make the difference and whose students perform better as a result.[4]

However, not all of those teachers "who work harder to make a difference and whose students perform better as a result" will be rewarded. Only teachers in the disciplines of mathematics and science need apply. We can generously surmise that Cuomo's only intent was to improve student performance in mathematics and science, but the exclusionary aspect of this program is likely to have a vastly different effect than what was intended.

The recently awarded MacArthur Fellows show evidence of balance in lauding great work in various areas of study. William Dichtel's "Genius Grant," awarded to him on the assembly of molecules into high surface-area networks, demonstrates an appreciation of the extraordinary science of Dichtel and his team at Cornell University.[5] Lorenz Studer's work on stem cell biology at Sloan-Kettering Cancer Center suggests that the breakthrough in "dopaminergic neurons" may have practical applications in cancer cure or prevention.[6]

Urban sociologist Matthew Desmond's work on the impact of eviction on the lives of the poor, Michelle Dorrance's work as a dancer and choreographer, LaToya Ruby Frazier's contributions to photography and video art, and Ta-Nehisi Coates's journalism reflect the diversity of these "Genius Grant" recipients and are all indicative of the value ascribed to these humanities scholars' contributions.[7]

Coates's book *Between the World and Me* changes the conversation once it is read, and Coates's questions and analysis help us to understand how racial inequality remains with us as a cultural and social cancer, just as lethal as those cancers that Dichtel is working on in science.

What is amazing about the MacArthur awards is the implicit understanding that incredibly significant advancements come into our lives from diverse areas and fields of study. There is a sense of balance in the concept of this type of recognition of the importance of the contributions of individuals across diverse areas of scholarship that is utterly lacking in the STEM proponents' mission and in the manner it is being carried out.

The MacArthur awards are a model of how to award individual achievement while lifting the whole discipline and culture. We do not have to reduce one area to bolster another.

Well-meaning people are working on perceived problems in education, but the gulf between intention and impact is wide indeed. In a recent article in *Scientific American*, author Melanie Tannenbaum stated, "I spend a lot of time talking with friends and colleagues about societal issues that we find meaningful and important. Racism. Sexism. Cultural sensitivity. Prejudice. Implicit biases. This is a line that we often find ourselves repeating: 'It's not about intent. It's about impact.'"[8]

The impact of current school reforms is and will continue to be harsh, perhaps insurmountable, unless the dialogue changes, the venture capital interests are removed from the equation, and the American people wake up to their new STEM, charter school landscape of deepening divides between those permanently ensconced in privilege and those in hopelessness.

NOTES

1. US Department of Education.
2. Robert Barnes, "Supreme Court Stops Use of Key Part of Voting Rights Act," *Washington Post* (June 25, 2013), accessed September 28, 2015, https://www.washingtonpost.com/politics/supreme-court-stops-use-of-key-part-of-voting-rights-act/2013/06/25/26888528-dda5-11e2-b197-f248b21f94c4_story.html.
3. Master Teacher Program, New York State Master Teacher, SUNY (2015), https://www.suny.edu/MasterTeacher/.
4. Ibid.
5. Katherine Brooks, "Meet the 2015 MacArthur Fellows," *Huffington Post* (September 9, 2015), accessed September 9, 2015, http://www.huffingtonpost.com/entry/macarthur-genius-grant-2015_5609fce7e4b0af3706dd9d96.
6. Brooks, "Meet the 2015 MacArthur Fellows."
7. Ibid.
8. Melanie Tannenbaum, "'But I Didn't Mean It!' Why It's So Hard to Prioritize Impacts over Intents," *Scientific American*, blog (October 14, 2013), accessed September 14, 2015, http://blogs.scientificamerican.com/psysociety/e2809cbut-i-didne28099t-mean-ite2809d-why-ite28099s-so-hard-to-prioritize-impacts-over-intents/.

FIFTEEN
Welcome the Subversive

Question authority, and you might be in trouble, land in detention or in jail, bankrupt, or much worse. Almost all progress in civilization, however, has been made by someone questioning and defying an authority or authorities.

In the current climate, anyone not falling into line with the STEM movement and demanding the opening of new charter schools, crying out that unions need to be destroyed and teachers have to be replaced is likely to be labeled as subversive at worst or lazy and uncooperative at best. Those of us raising questions about these decisions should welcome the titles. All of the people on the list here were labeled subversives, at one point in history, by those around them. If we dare to question power, money interests, and authority, we are in good company.

Introducing the subversive:
Welcome,

Socrates
Plato
Copernicus
Hypatia of Alexandria
Galileo
Leonardo da Vinci
Jesus Christ
Isaac Newton
Marie Curie
Thomas Jefferson
Henry David Thoreau
Abraham Lincoln
Sigmund Freud
Friedrich Nietzsche

Charles Darwin
Victoria Woodhull
Albert Einstein
Nelson Mandela
Trưng Trắc and Trưng Nhị
Virginia Apgar
Dorothy Day
Thomas Merton
Aung San Suu Kyi
Malala Yousafzai
John Nash

The list is far too long and subjective (and purposely in random order), but anyone who appears on it introduced something that seemed threatening to those in authority positions at the time.

"[B]y exploring how great thinkers struggled and often went astray, we gain perspective on the initial strangeness of ideas,"[1] wrote Dana Goldstein in her book *The Teacher Wars: A History of America's Most Embattled Profession*. Each person on this list introduced something strange, even frightening, to people at the time.

Perhaps the term "divergent thinking" will unsettle people less than "subversive," with its heavy burden of negative connotation, but Galileo's ideas were subversive, dangerous, and threatening to the authorities who claimed—and everyone accepted under threat of death—the idea that the earth was the center of the universe. It seems ridiculous to us now that these ideas were so hostile to the way people framed their worldviews. Although Galileo had to apologize for his science and correct theorizing in order to save his life, his legacy of doubt created the possibility of another path not only for the Earth but thinking in general.

Before human beings create or innovate, they have already removed themselves from the mainstream thinking of their time. There is no one formula for creative innovation, but following standard procedures and protocol is unlikely to lead to something new, unless by the randomness of an accident introduced from an outside source.

Scientist Frank Wilczek recommends the "deeply subversive" in education in order to challenge ourselves and move beyond whatever accepted thinking clogs our path: "Do not accept limitations. Struggle to attempt different ways of viewing things. Doubt your perceptions. Be suspicious of authority."[2] Wilczek is looking for the beautiful in logic, in thinking, in human existence. Of course, his last piece of advice causes the most trouble.

"Authority," as noted in his book, may represent any number of entities, including the state, political leaders, administrators, even teachers, as authority figures in a classroom. We should all welcome the challenge and be unafraid of questions. True education lies in getting students to go to that place of doubt and to make the effort to formulate their own questions.

We should return to one of the great pedagogical thinkers and writers, John Dewey, whom Dana Goldstein quotes in the epigraph to her powerful work *The Teacher Wars: A History of America's Most Embattled Profession*:

> It is ... advisable that the teacher should understand, and even be able to criticize, the general principles upon which the whole educational system is formed and administered. He is not like a private soldier in an army, expected merely to obey, or like a cog in a wheel, expected merely to respond to and transmit external energy; he must be an intelligent medium of action.[3]

Dewey's wise words are as relevant today as they were in 1895. If we are going to help students make that leap in order to formulate questions rather than just compliantly respond with the predicted, or scripted, answers, if we want our children to think for themselves, as we claim, we need to be less afraid of the subversive and the new, less afraid of failing in order to learn, less afraid to question power and political entities that dictate.

Education reform has been shifted on its axis by too many people who do not particularly welcome questions. This should trouble every American far beyond the boundaries of conversations about education or public school reforms.

NOTES

1. Goldstein, *Teacher Wars*, 3.
2. Wilczek, *Beautiful Question*, 57.
3. Goldstein, epigraph to *Teacher Wars*.

SIXTEEN

Insights from the Humanities

How is something new created? What is behind the thought processes that allow human beings to conceive of things that were not there before, in some text, example, or laboratory? At times, we are confronted with the radically new when we stumble upon it accidentally. When we are engaged in science and mathematics in a laboratory or working out a complex equation, we come across formulas that do not add up unless we consider the absence rather than the presence.

Contemporary American poet Mark Doty suggests in his essay "Souls on Ice" that metaphors are the "advance guard of the mind," leading us to places we did not even know we needed to go.[1] As if the discovery is awaiting the catch up of our minds. It is intriguing to consider that a path already lies ahead for innovation; we just have to be willing to venture out without the road map, go in another direction, and imagine possibility.

Conversely, these insights could also be seen as aberrations, problems that produce solutions. One such description of the paradoxical oddity of the creative process is metaphorically expressed by mathematician Donald Newman in his comments on the brilliant insights of Noble Prize-winning mathematician John Nash in *The Essential John Nash*: "Everyone else would climb a peak by looking for a path somewhere on the mountain. Nash would climb another mountain altogether and from that distant peak would shine a searchlight back on the first peak."[2]

Newman suggests that Nash's approach was so radically different from his colleagues that he was likely to shed light on the problem even if he did not solve it. He was looking at the problem even when he was engaged in other activities or from "another mountain."

On May 23, 2015, Nash and his wife Alicia were tragically killed in a car accident while riding in a taxi in New Jersey, and his stunning successes in light of his schizophrenia were again recalled in the news and conversations everywhere. He was just returning from Norway to accept another prize in mathematics, and the strangeness and abruptness of the tragedy only reinforced the random chaos we are confronted with each day.

It is not enough to be hugely successful in this world. We also need to confront all of the questions that we are compelled to construct around our mortality. Nash was immensely successful as a mathematician, but no one would propose that we need to be schizophrenic in order to be more innovative. It is reasonable to assume, however, that we need to examine the problem from other positions, through another lens, or a place that is at once foreign and exciting, from a position where failure is at least as likely as success.

Contributions and critical importance of the humanities should require no defense, but in this environment, we feel compelled to point out what should be obvious. The way forward, as well as the record of the way back, can be traced to the searching mind, the origin of every course of study in the humanities.

New Yorker writer, esteemed literary critic, and Harvard English Professor Louis Menand offers insight into the creative process, as well as his thoughts on the value of a liberal arts education, in an address given at Bowdoin College:

> Liberal education does teach useful things. . . . The first is methodology, protocols for inquiry. Liberal education teaches you how to assemble, interpret and evaluate data, how to turn information into knowledge. . . . This gives a clue to the value-added potential of liberal education. What your professors mean by "thinking" is the ability to see around the corner of what is already out there, what is already known, what everyone takes for granted—the ability, really, to see that there *is* a corner at the end of our little street. That's something that most people are never able to see.[3]

In a few precise words, Menand managed to puncture a rather large hole in the STEM school reform movement without even trying.

He also provides a "clue" as to where innovative thinkers are looking (seeing "around the corner"). In other words, innovators are seeing something no one else can see, and Menand credits the liberal arts education with fostering that almost undefinable ability in human beings. It may be discovered in music, art, and language interactions that provide the disturbance, the agitation, to allow us to see with new eyes.

NOTES

1. Mark Doty, "Souls on Ice," Poets.org (July 18, 2000), accessed September 30, 2015, https://www.poets.org/poetsorg/text/souls-ice.

2. Newman, *The Essential John Nash*, edited by Harold W. Kuhn and Sylvia Nasar.

3. Louis Menand, "What's It All About?" Bowdoin College, Bowdoin.edu. (October 22, 2010), accessed October 28, 2015), http://www.bowdoin.edu/news/archives/1bowdoincampus/007902.shtml.

SEVENTEEN
Allow Every Teacher to Engineer Reform

If we want school reform that changes lives, alters how we function in schools, raises student performance, and improves student skills and products, we need to rethink how reform is created. The tradition of top-down is not only ineffective but often damaging to good programs, good schools, successful teachers, and students. Federal and state mandates, state and federal administrative policy directives, threats and intimidation through funding or denial of funding have proven to be the arbiters of mediocrity and/or poor student performance.

Perhaps we could try another approach entirely. ESSA legislation may allow room for at least a discussion of this type of teacher experimentation if state and local district administrators permit something really revolutionary in education to occur. Where opportunity exists, educators need to be ready and willing to take advantage of an opening.

Teachers should know through experience that if their students are involved in the design of the product or the lesson, those students perform at a higher level with less oversight needed. (See Dafoe's book *Breaking Open the Box: A Guide for Creative Techniques to Improve Academic Writing and Generate Critical Thinking*.) Yet educators continue to provide too much for students largely because the punitive models set up for educators are focused on grading and judgment, evaluation of the student and assessment of the teacher through students' test scores. Like building a high rise with a cracking foundation, the specifications for this construct are inherently flawed.

Staff development varies from district to district but consists largely of "experts" coming into a building to lecture an entire staff for a single day. The problems with this long-established model are many, but to break it down into simplest terms: the design employed on school staff development days seldom, if ever, models good teaching practice. From the voices of hundreds of educators in different districts, staff development days feel like either a vacation day, a tedious repetition of information they already know or have, or demeaning exercises in futility. Administrative intentions are good, so what goes wrong?

In nearly every instance, staff development providers are intelligent people with interesting ideas, so why is the standard presentation result the opposite of what is intended? The first, and most significant, reason is that teachers are not involved with the content and not particularly engaged during the presentation.

Ask teachers what they need to improve practice, and they will tell you or they will offer suggestions. The problem is that every teacher—just as every student—does not need the same prescription. Being lectured to for hours, while sitting passively, is typically not a good recipe for intellectual stimulation. One particular lecturer punctuated his hours' long presentation with occasional shouting/screaming in what could only be termed a childish impulse to wake up his audience. Of course, it felt like insult and verbal assault to many of the faculty in attendance.

Why has public school staff development been arranged in this one-day lecture presentation manner? It is, quite simply, the most efficient way to reach an entire faculty with one message on one given, pre-determined day. Expediency and efficiency take precedence over effectiveness.

In some respects, this is a similar problem to what students experience to varying degrees during many of their school days. Lecture-based classes allow students to fall into a passivity that mirrors sleep, but a large amount of material is covered. We should all know better.

Analyzing the problem begins with a look at the natural impulse for expediency. There is an abundance of evidence of administration at every level—federal, state, local districts—choosing expediency over proven efficacy: a too-rapid roll out of severely flawed testing aligned to the Common Core, the Common Core mandate and adoption before vetting problems, language, student diversity, and socioeconomic conditions, as well as other issues at play in a national curriculum, are just a few examples of this wide-spread practice.

Suppose we make a collective decision to choose effectiveness over expediency? What would such a model look like, and how could we guarantee positive results for students? If it is all really about students and only about helping improve skills, we might approach the problems with greater creativity. We might be willing to set aside politics—the fears that American students are in whatever position on global testing—until after we consider what that testing really measures and its worth.

Real accomplishment and innovation often comes about as a result, or even a byproduct, of failures. Thomas Edison is noted to have said, "I have not failed. I've just found 10,000 ways that won't work."[1] Students and teachers need this freedom to find "ways that won't work" in order to discover what works incredibly well.

Who knows the students better than their teachers and their parents? Begin with classroom teachers, with some input from students and parents. Interdisciplinary teams of teachers, selected students, and community members could be tasked with goals identified and prioritized by administration—at the federal, state, and local levels.

Goal-setting and coordination should, of course, take place at the highest levels, but the practice of how to design effective models for meeting those goals is best determined by the day-to-day practitioners in the classrooms with input from various other groups. Creating and designing are exciting processes and will engage teachers as well as students.

By way of one example, an interdisciplinary high school team discusses the skills and concepts in their specific content areas where common ground could be found.

Let's say the physical education teacher is planning a canoe trip down a nearby river. The English teacher has students read a small section of Thoreau's *Walden* and Annie Dillard's "Living Like Weasels." This history teacher works with students on the concept of American transcendentalism, and the environmental science teacher plans a field lab on rivers in cooperation with the physical education teacher.

Students could also measure current and distance for a mathematics' teacher. Then the students could write about the experience like a contemporary Thoreau, using their detailed observations and field notes. They could also compose or play music or draw, paint, or sculpt art projects related to thematic ideas uncovered.

Would students be engaged? Yes. Would they learn a great deal while analyzing, processing, measuring, calculating, exercising, synthesizing, reading, writing, creating, and discussing? Undoubtedly. What prevents this type of revolutionary and exciting education from taking place? Scheduling—one of the most important factors in education often ends up missing the bus.

There would also be concerns from content area teachers and administrators that too much time was spent on an interdisciplinary unit and a specific curriculum could not be fully covered by the end of the semester of the year. Yet what difference does it make how much is covered if the students only truly assimilate a tiny fraction of the curriculum?

Again, this is where state or federal testing hampers rather than simply measures learning. Reform policy could require that each district submit their testing measurements but allow districts to choose what those measurements would look like. While students would still take the SATs and/or ACTs for college, the interdisciplinary lessons and higher level of engagement and greater degree of creative control would likely lead to better standardized tests results, as well. Students who are interested in scholarly pursuits and proud of their accomplishments generally do a better job on assessments.

Administrators could help facilitate and/or design more flexible school schedules for students and teachers to permit both the innovative approaches, as well as assessment consultations with teachers and peers. We can imagine some administrators stating that this "would be a nightmare to try and schedule," but only if we continue to think about schedules and classrooms in a traditional manner.

Imagine a high school or junior high in which the required subjects could be met by the student deciding which units to take rather than which course is required each year? In other words, environmental science might be part of a senior unit, and biology might be part of a unit a freshman could take. This type of interdisciplinary approach would probably be easier to accomplish in an elementary school, but it can be done at the secondary level, as well.

All of the ideas presented here—and countless others—are those of teachers who want to help "engineer" education regeneration and be innovative creators, not passive receptacles of reform. Students feel that same kind of urgency to be engaged, create, make new discoveries while learning. We have the will but not yet the authority to give them this gift.

NOTE

1. Thomas Edison, Goodreads quotes, accessed January 6, 2016, http://www.goodreads.com/author/quotes/3091287.Thomas_A_Edison.

EIGHTEEN
The Waste Land Revisited

> We will find a way eventually to live with our inborn turmoil and perhaps find pleasure in viewing it as the primary source of our creativity.
> —E. O. Wilson in *The Meaning of Human Existence*.[1]

If the poet T. S. Eliot had not adopted the mantle of the Fisher King as our guide through his seminal poem *The Waste Land*, we might still be lingering there. As an archetypal symbol and spiritual entity, the Fisher King can move between realms, between the living and the dead, can assume another sex, can heal the wounds of others, even if he/she cannot heal his/her own grievous wounds.[2]

In our contemporary scene and purported "waste land in American education," however, we have only those making policies and decisions—the business CEO and the politician—leading us. In this parody, our guides have no knowledge of a spiritual realm, nor are they cognizant of the degradation of humanity around them.

REVISITING ELIOT'S *THE WASTE LAND* AS PARODY AND HOMAGE

April is still the cruelest month
because that is "when taxes are due," according to our CEO guide
who thinks and speaks in prose rather than poetry
through this "Waste Land" that is public education, according to his rhetoric.
Unfortunately for children, however, this proclaimed "waste land"
has no spiritual guide, no Tiresias, but rather, politicians and businessmen
to set the tone and the pace; we move endlessly in a circular, worn path.
"There are profits to be made out of this destruction," our guide smiles.
Without T. S. Eliot's other worldly Fisher King at our sides, we are reduced
to follow the lead of a Third, not a Shadow who walks beside us,

but a self-important politician who owes his recent election to generous campaign donations
of our other double, the CEO, who muses neither upon the king nor his father,
nor those who came before him, considering the fact he has dismissed history,
the CEO gorging upon the "$788.7 billion market in K–12 education,"
to say nothing of how high it could go
if he incorporates the lucrative college market.
Testing and tests will be sold at a premium,
available only from said CEO, the agent creating data-driven,
incessantly talking without recognition or pity:
we are thirsty, and there is no water.
Children are asking for water.

We still open our mouths to utter words but not about when we were children
or about children who are seldom part of this conversation,
in strange and hostile mountains;
rather, we learn about commodities and reducing scrap.
We are left with, "only vanity [which] requires no response,"
making a "welcome of indifference" about real children,
indifference to poverty and the multilayered challenges to learning.

When we finally get in a word to ask,
"What grows out of this rubbish?"
Meaning, "How are we supposed to get rid of scrap
when these parts you speak of are the children?"
We are greeted with a look of incredulity
as our CEO/politician guides have morphed into one entity
with the businessman now owning the politician through campaign
donations and PACS; our CEO suggests that rubbish removal
is lucrative and he could make millions
if we just reduce overhead expenses, while implicating
all of us in the excising of children and their teachers.

There is no tenderness here, no impatient forbearance.
We will hear no sirens call, jazz riffs, or any other music.

And there is still no relief and no water.
There is no clairvoyant, no Madame Sosostris,
but a speculator proclaiming,
"Fear the Market devalued."

Everything seems unreal, and the crowd moves in unison not
terribly unlike the zombies in pick-your-version movie, television,
computer-generated mind-numbing "entertainment"
designed to keep us quiet and unaware of our thirst.

When we ask, "Do you know nothing? Do you see nothing?
Do you remember nothing?" our CEO admits
he knows no past, recalls no history, reflection

never his strong suit, he says, buttoning the top button.
There is only the present and the possibility of the future
in which a killing in the markets is tangible in statistical form,
and certainly there is money to be made in education.
There are tests to be marketed and sold,
so that every child will take many tests
ordered from his company each year.
"Hurry up? It's time," he says,
leaving out the polite entreaty, "please."

"The sound of horns and motors" are music to his ears.
No, there is no Tiresias, no androgynous prophet nor prophetess,
only vanity and greed rising and personified
in the guise of our guide.

We do not go to Athens or Carthage because history does not exist
for him, and so he blinds our view of it, cuts us off from our past,
and we begin to drown, the paradox not lost on us,
but utterly bewildering to our CEO guide.
"How can we possibly drown in a dry wasteland?"
He asks, sweating profusely while still calculating
his expenses and potential losses.
Oblivious to parched lips,
Oblivious to paradoxically rising but deadly waters,
the politician/CEO drinks from a flask
but offers us none of the martini in his hand.
In his waistcoat, he tucks a bottle of Vodka,
for just such occasions but says it is only for emergencies,
unaware of lolling tongues, cracked lips around him.

"Fragments," we remark. "There is no peace."
"War and education are profitable," the CEO/politician remarks
with gory glory in his blue eyes.
When we desperately ask our guide again,
"Do you know nothing? Do you see nothing?"
We are greeted with a mocking sneer.
"There is nothing to see. You have no history,"
he remarks, "There are the Dow and Nasdaq and S&P.
They are rising with our invasions."

We look bleary-eyed over the desolate landscape,
hearing no Thunder Gods or commands from a spiritual realm,
and walk on choking on dust, weary travelers into endless night.

Our CEO/politician turns and says, "I will not give any more to the needy.
I will eliminate welfare and social services and public schooling.
I will control the money and the tax rates and charter schools.
I will not sympathize with the poor, destitute, or disadvantaged,
or, for that matter, the middle class or immigrant families."

We hear his commands as he rolls his nakedness in money,
bathing in greed.
There is no water and no relief.

Empty of its children and all forms of humane life,
all the world goes dark,
and all the world grows loud
before continued darkness.

NOTES

1. Wilson, 34.
2. T. S. Eliot, *The Waste Land*, Bartleby.com, Great Books Online (1993–2015), accessed February 27, 2015, http://www.bartleby.com/201/1.html.

NINETEEN
Creating Meaningful, Lasting Reform

The first step in creating meaningful education reform is to acknowledge the complexity of the cultural, social, and economic issues that have profoundly causative effects on students' achievements and ability to learn, as well as demonstrate their learning. The second step involves working to address the underlying socioeconomic issues through progressive, but carefully thought-out, policies. Only then we can begin to tackle problems inherent in a public school model.

The third step is to recognize that across-the-board "solutions" to problems in education are ridiculous. Schools and students are performing in vastly different arenas, and the results reflect that dichotomy, as well as state, regional, local, and family economics.

Reform is not impossible, and positive movement is not hopeless. Are there steps that can be taken to help improve education? Of course, and improving teacher training programs in college is one of those steps. Other logical steps follow:

- Reframe the STEM acronym. Perhaps a word like "ENLIGHTENENT" works better in that it is focused on the wake-up call for "the searching mind," and its many letters allow for greater inclusivity.
- Embrace project-based learning as a cross-discipline approach for the purpose of creating transformative learning, higher student engagement, and encouraging the "searching mind."
- Encourage, promote, and fund flexible schedules (or built in "January Plan," such as some colleges offer) and sufficient time in the day for students to meet with teachers across disciplines for intensive discussions and project review.
- Encourage, promote, and fund reduced course loads for teachers, which would allow for additional planning and coordination of students' cross-discipline projects, labs, and intensive study.

- Encourage, promote, and fund professional mentoring—not evaluation—for staff to allow teachers who have successfully managed to oversee and evaluate students on successful cross-discipline projects to work with other teachers who have no or little experience in this type of learning.
- Encourage and provide funding from local, state, and federal governments to keep public school staffing levels high enough to support this approach to meaningful scholarship on a continuing basis, not as a model or show-piece but as part of the regular offering for all students, from every background.
- Allow for and provide more structured opportunities for classroom teachers' voices to be heard in the reform process.
- Allow students' and their parents' voices to be heard in this process of educational reform.

WHAT WOULD A MEANINGFUL PROJECT LOOK LIKE FOR STUDENTS? A NARRATIVE

Chloe came into class one morning, her eyes moist with tears and her face marked by red splotches. When she was privately asked what was wrong, she said that her grandmother had been diagnosed with Alzheimer's and didn't remember Chloe anymore.

Chloe did not want to be in school because, at that critical moment, education appeared to be peripheral, if not irrelevant, yet, as her English teacher, I had just read an article in *Scientific American* that discussed Alzheimer's, and after I told her about Gary Stix's article "Lifting the Curse of Alzheimer's," Chloe was transformed into a curious human being with a "searching mind."

This scenario would be a perfect one to introduce the idea of meaningful project-based learning, which should not be mistaken for some silly, forced exercise created by a teacher to look good in an annual performance review or a student looking to get out of scholarly work. Project-based learning that grows out of the student's need and genuine interest may be one of the most powerful strategies for learning new information, retaining it, and applying that knowledge to life and/or a career path.

How might such a project be set up? Chloe would begin by discussing her interest in Alzheimer's disease with her teachers, in this case her AP biology and AP English teachers, before gathering a reading list and research materials with the aid of her teachers, if needed. A rubric would be shared by Chloe and her teachers, in order for everyone involved in the project to understand what was being measured or evaluated at the end of the project.

After an initial review of the literature, Chloe would outline her project and meet with her teachers again to discuss the parameters of her project and to make sure that it was both meaningful and manageable. Then Chloe would use her project time (whatever the school allows) to create a project that could involve active research on her part, with her grandmother as part of her study or an essay about the effects of the disease on families, as well as individuals with Alzheimer's.

Chloe would meet at least once halfway through the project with her teachers to make sure that she was not making major errors or getting off the topic track. Then Chloe could present her paper to a review board with her teachers. Chloe learns about the disease, thinks deeply and critically, analyzes and synthesizes across multiple sources of media, and presents her findings or discoveries in a coherent, engaging manner.

Sounds great—meaningful, engaging, and challenging to the student, and learning is taking place precisely at the moment when Chloe wanted to turn away from education. How might Chloe's experience work for any interested student? And how would this type of learning change the educational system? It is worth repeating here because it is attainable and viable:

- A reduced course load for teachers, which would allow for interdisciplinary planning and coordination of projects.
- A flexible schedule and sufficient time in the day for students to meet with teachers for intensive one-on-one discussion and review.
- Professional mentoring for staff to allow teachers who have successfully managed to oversee and evaluate students on successful projects to work with other teachers who have no experience in this type of learning.
- Sufficient funding from the local, state, and federal governments to keep staffing levels high enough to support this approach to meaningful scholarship on a continuing basis (not as a model but as part of the regular offering for all students).

Sound familiar? What is required here for student success is difficult but possible and deserves reiteration. Politicians need to step away from the quick and easy, but frequently hollow, sound bites about education. Policymakers should employ seasoned classroom educators and administrators in the process of analysis, and local districts need the input of teachers, parents, students, and communities as they work together for positive change.

TWENTY
Convergence of Poetry/Science

An Interdisciplinary Approach to Teaching and Learning

On the evening of October 14, 2015, in Syracuse, New York, members of the audience were treated to an evening with author and Harvard University professor, Stephen Greenblatt, who took them through a lecture that was all at once historical, literary, filled with scientific information, as well as visual arts, and mathematically and linguistically precise.

Greenblatt's lecture, a part of the Rosamond Gifford Lecture Series, offered a perfect melding of typically diverse areas of study, vastly enriching the audience's understanding not only of Shakespeare's tragedy *King Lear* but printing technology, English history, Darwin's theory of evolution, the sociology and psychology of parenting and aging, all through a narrative thread. It was, in fact, a perfect model for education.

Granted, acquiring the kind of deep knowledge of numerous subjects that Greenblatt has is not easy, but whereas Greenblatt stood alone on that stage, other educators may stand with colleagues. The idea that we need an interdisciplinary approach to teaching and learning is neither new nor radical in any way, but its implementation has proven to be particularly difficult—and not because teachers are unwilling.

First, it must be acknowledged that this kind of teaching and learning is difficult and takes great care and preparation on the part of the teachers or professors. This accession also requires a support system that provides continuing education for the teacher, administration that allows the teacher to try new ways of looking at learning, and students who are prepared to learn. Further, there must be resolve that all academic disciplines have value because we learn and experience through interconnections. This interdisciplinary venture may require more than one or even multiple teachers in a classroom.

Certainly, teachers who are well versed across multiple disciplines will be better able to create this experience for students. The approach also suggests that continual coordination and meetings between teachers in diverse areas may be of great benefit. What is also suggested is a change in teacher preparation. Any or all of these resolutions are possible if we have the will, but they require time and funding in order to improve our educational offering to students.

There is not one perfect model of education. There is not one template that will solve the problems we associate with education when a child does not learn or struggles to advance. If we begin by admitting it is complicated and difficult, at least we are starting with honesty. If we admit that some students will falter because their lives are so fractured and they are not yet ready to learn, we have at long last recognized some societal issues that powerfully impact education.

Educators want to make their students' lives better. This is by and large true of the vast majority of people who go into education, which is not the kind of profession that attracts venture capitalists. Educators spend years in school and want to be successful as teachers or professors, desiring the same levels of success for their students. Where we go wrong is not lack of caring, work ethic, or resolve.

How do we begin after removing the politicians and businessmen from policy directives? Encourage teachers through something as simple as praise and allowing them to try new strategies and ideas without penalty. Allow teachers, as well as students, to occasionally fail without consequences because we all learn at that edge, the one where failure of an experiment, a wrong note, a disastrous word choice, or a missing formula takes us to a new level of understanding. Perhaps it starts with just two teachers, a chemistry and an English teacher, or a foreign language and an English teacher, or an art teacher and mathematics teacher, getting together to discuss the convergence of their disciplines and how to make that manifest in a classroom.

What happens when a chemistry teacher and English teacher get together to talk?

Molecular Spectroscopy

Corresponding to Collisions
It's simple, really:
We're all looking for truth.
Searching inside energy, inside metaphors
where poetry, physics, philosophy, chemistry, history,
mathematics, the arts, and astronomy collide and change
in the light we hold them.

Euclid, Coleridge, Newton, Calvino, Rayleigh, Neruda—
at one end of a wavelength of intellectual light,
our students scattered at the other,

> but don't stop from mixing science, history,
> mathematics, poetry, science, poetry
> symmetrically, of course.
> You've got it; it's deliberate: chiasmus, too.
> Between matter and energy, the matter, a pun
> created to challenge, see how concepts resonate,
> another play on the way we function, the way we see;
> so, the scattering corresponds to molecular spectroscopy:
> we're absorbed in what may have been born
> in Newton's optics, but we find our way poetically
> in this energy transfer from teacher to student,
> student to student, student to teacher, teacher to teacher,
> our processes dynamic, resonant frequency resonates
> within our rational, artistic, philosophical souls,
> as well as revealing truth in white light.

The poem was written by an English teacher for a chemistry teacher's presentation, resulting in a high level of interest among the chemistry teachers considering ways to "write across curricula."

Suppose students were asked to compose poems about chemistry, or chemistry students played with language about their science in concept journals? The idea that students should only write in an English class is pretty absurd when you stop to think about it, and the idea that students should be exposed to principles in science only in a science class is equally ridiculous.

What would school look like if we were less divided by specialty and more focused on areas of student interest, charging our students to become deeply involved in scholarly projects developed by students—not teachers, parents, or politicians—according to their interests?

$P(A)\ P(A \cup B)\ E(X\ /\ Y)$

Could we ask students to use terms from science and mathematics in history and English?

Find the mathematical terms, or better yet, ask students to create a short critique of motive in *Hamlet* (or any other work of literature), using terms found in mathematics:

> A function more suitable to Hamlet's suits of woe—
> in which the angle of suspicion
> implies derivative of his Uncle's guilt—
> although no less obtuse than
> Gertrude's supposed sorrow

Ask students to play with language in a science course or consider science concepts in an English or foreign language class.

These intertextual and cross-disciplinary relationships already exist, but we seldom encourage students to experiment in this manner, primarily because we are concerned about testing and student outcomes. These types of playful, yet complex, writing activities, however, will likely yield far better testing results once students are asked to express what they have learned on better tests.

Discussions and activities of this sort do not require setting up charter schools or more testing, but simply require a willingness to try something new without threats or penalties looming over the heads of teachers and students. The idea is to generate ideas!

"Mathematical symbols and language undergo a Darwinian sort of evolution," wrote Alice M. Dean, in her paper on "Symbol and Meaning in Mathematics"[1] In one sentence, Dean addresses analysis in English (language and language symbols), mathematics (symbols), and science (Darwin's *On the Origin of Species*), bringing them together to allow for us to consider interrelationships and a far deeper understanding of each concept.

Making the connection explicit, Dean elaborated, "As new ideas are discovered, mathematicians introduce new symbols and language to describe them."[2] This should not be strange territory. As educators, we are all engaged in the realm of symbols and specialized language.

Good science cannot happen solely in a laboratory, and good literature is not created in a vacuum. New ideas arise out of these deep and playful dives into other disciplines. The evidence is all around us if we open our eyes to the possibilities, as suggested by Yoko Ogawa's text *The Housekeeper and the Professor*, in which readers may, like her protagonist, "swoop down on the numbers, like a kingfisher catching the glint of sunlight on the fish's fin."[3]

How should we promote this deep diving in schools? Open the discussion to allow educators and students not simply a seat at the table but a prominent role in the design. Although school districts attempt this, the results fall short because, in too many cases, the outcomes have already been determined, and the assigned roles at the table are merely decoration.

Make sure every school has funding for texts and great models in every discipline and across diverse fields of study, relegating testing to the reduced role of measurement—not punishment for student or teacher. Demonstrate the belief that every discipline, every student, and every teacher has value. Encourage teachers in different specialties to work together and provide time for the interactions to be meaningful.

The equation resulting from good schools and well-educated students requires enthusiastic teachers who believe they have a voice and a role in the design of curricula and students who are willing and capable of participating in their education. The second part of the construct means we have to look at and address social ills that cause such disruption in students' lives.

Although public school districts do make this effort to design and implement "pyramids of intervention," they infrequently follow all the way through to completion, allowing the troubled student to reenter. The equation also asks all of us to be willing to listen to each other. Listening to each other suggests that politicians might do well to listen to educators before making yet another misguided pronouncement.

Time is the key to success in many of these strategies—time for educators to work out new ideas and professional practices—as well as space to implement new concepts in teaching. Rather than prosecute teachers, putting them on trial for their students' failings or students' inability to perform at optimum levels on multiple tests—often given on the same day—suppose we support students and teachers who are struggling by giving them additional help.

A suggestion given by students, but not heeded, has been separate test days, so students are not overwhelmed and physically, to say nothing of mentally, exhausted.

A great teacher can take material that a student would not normally be interested in and turn that material into gold. But a great teacher does not instantly materialize. A great teacher takes time and practice, continuing education, and positive feedback without threat or intimidation.

We are capable of creating a public school system that encourages amazing teaching and makes our schools places where students feel the freedom to risk failure. Only in risking failure do we really learn. The current reform movement allows no place for the most natural and normal part of learning and that is the stumble, the error, the mistake from which we gain so much, learn to pick ourselves up, and try again with new insights. Any professional in any field of study can attest to these missteps necessary for success.

Challenge yourself to discover the mathematics in Samuel Taylor Coleridge's poem. Here we find a marriage of poetry and mathematics in perfect symmetry.

A Mathematical Problem

(on Euclid's proposition)

> This is now—this was erst,
> Proposition the first—and Problem the first.
> I.
> On a given finite Line
> Which must no way incline;
> To describe an equi—
> —lateral Tri—
> —A, N, G, L, E.
> Now let A. B.
> Be the given line
> Which must no way incline;
> The great Mathematician
> Makes this Requisition,
> That we describe an Equi—
> —lateral Tri—

—angle on it:
Aid us, Reason—aid us, Wit!
II.
From the centre A. at the distance A. B.
Describe the circle B. C. D.
At the distance B. A. from B. the centre
The round A. C. E. to describe boldly venture.
(Third Postulate see.)
And from the point C.
In which the circles make a pother
Cutting and slashing one another,
Bid the straight lines a journeying go,
C. A., C. B. those lines will show.
To the points, which by A. B. are reckon'd,
And postulate the second
For Authority ye know.
A. B. C.
Triumphant shall be
An Equilateral Triangle,
Not Peter Pindar carp, not Zoilus can wrangle.
III.
Because the point A. is the centre
Of the circular B. C. D.
And because the point B. is the centre
Of the circular A. C. E.
A. C. to A. B. and B. C. to B. A.
Harmoniously equal forever must stay;
Then C. A. and B. C.
Both extend the kind hand
To the basis, A. B.
Unambitiously join'd in Equality's Band.
But to the same powers, when two powers are equal,
My mind forbodes the sequel;
My mind does some celestial impulse teach,
And equalises each to each.
Thus C. A. with B. C. strikes the same sure alliance,
That C. A. and B. C. had with A. B. before;
And in mutual affiance,
None attempting to soar
Above another,
The unanimous three
C. A. and B. C. and A. B.
All are equal, each to his brother,
Preserving the balance of power so true:
Ah! The line would the proud Autocratorix do!
At taxes impending not Britain would tremble,
Nor Prussia struggle her fear to dissemble;
Nor the Mah'met-sprung Wight,
The great Mussulman

Convergence of Poetry/Science 111

> Would stain his Divan
> With Urine the soft-flowing daughter of Fright.
> IV.
> But rein your stallion in, too daring Nine!
> Should Empires bloat the scientific line?
> Or with dishevell'd hair all madly do ye run
> For transport that your task is done?
> For done it is—the cause is tried!
> And Proposition, gentle Maid,
> Who soothly ask'd stern Demonstration's aid,
> Has prov'd her right, and A. B. C.
> Of Angles three
> Is shown to be of equal side;
> And now our weary steed to rest in fine,
> 'Tis rais'd upon A. B. the straight, the given line.

Have fun discovering and analyzing the mathematical principles in William Butler Yeats's poem:

An Irish Airman Foresees His Death

Balance or symmetry and antithesis; mathematically balanced; 16 lines; square root of 16 is 4 (4 metrical feet in a line—tetrameter); 64 metrical feet; square root of 64 is 8. Each of the 16 lines consists of two equal halves. Half of 16 is 8, and there are or 32 halves in the poem, and 4 times 8 equals 32; there are 2 spondees; there are 2 trochees, and 2 + 2 = 4 feet in each line. The rhyme scheme is also mathematically balanced:

I know that *I shall meet* my fate,	(4 iambs or iambic tetrameter)
Somewhere among the clouds above;	(4 iambs)
Those that I fight I do not hate,	(4 feet: 1 trochee and 3 iambs)
Those that I guard *I do not love*;	(4 feet: 1 trochee and 3 iambs)
My country is Kiltartan Cross,	(4 feet: 3 iambs and 1 spondee)
My countrymen Kiltartan's poor,	(4 feet: 3 iambs and 1 spondee)
No likely end could bring them loss	(4 feet: 4 iambs)
Or leave them *happier than before*.	(4 feet: 4 iambs)
Nor law, *nor duty* bade me fight,	(4 feet: 4 iambs)
Nor public men, *nor cheering crowds*,	(4 feet: 4 iambs)
A lonely impulse of delight	(4 feet: 4 iambs)
Drove to this *tumult in* the clouds;	(4 feet: 3 iambs and 1 trochee)
<u>I balanced all</u>, *brought all to mind*,	(4 feet: 4 iambs)
The years to come seemed waste of breath,	(4 feet: 4 iambs)
A waste of breath the *years behind*	(4 feet: 4 iambs)
In balance with this life, *this death*.	(4 feet: 4 iambs)

ABAB CDCD EFEF GHGH into 4 quatrains of rhyme. It appears Yeats loved mathematics too.

Using the symbols and language of mathematics, students may explore poetry and literature, music and science.

Create a poem, using only mathematical terms or symbols: Here are a few to start you thinking and writing:

$|x|$ $\mathbb{Q}$

$|-4|$ is 4   Rational numbers

Factorial (n!) $P(A \cup B)$ probability of events union

Figure 20.1.

NOTES

1. Alice M. Dean, "Symbol and Meaning in Mathematics," Skidmore College (May 26, 1995), accessed November 20, 2014, https://www.skidmore.edu/~adean/papers/D_96_SymbolsInMath.pdf.
2. Dean, "Symbol and Meaning in Mathematics."
3. Yoko Ogawa, *The Housekeeper and the Professor*, (New York: Picador Edition, 2009).

TWENTY-ONE
Raining Poets

This essay was originally delivered by Nancy A. Dafoe as a speech to the newly inducted members of a chapter of the National Honor Society on a Wednesday evening in April 2015. The text version of the speech has been abbreviated by removing the poetic words from the poets, in respect to copyright law. The students, however, were able to hear the actual, powerful, and evocative words of the poets that remarkable evening.

Let me preface my remarks tonight with these statements: I love science. I love mathematics. And I believe in each and every one of you, in your astonishing capabilities to fly. Not long ago, I was flying in an airplane and happened to look down as we passed over a beautiful bridge spanning the Potomac River, and I thought how remarkable that bridge is, how perfect the symmetry, a concept we find in science, math, and poetry.

Considering science, there is simply no way to talk or write articulately or coherently about black holes and dozens of other topics in physics and the highest levels of mathematics without incorporating the language of poetry: the metaphor. Tonight, I'm taking you on a metaphoric journey, and we will see not where we will end but where we will arrive.

It starts like a magic realism scene: raining all morning, threatening to continue in that vein, a bleed out; cold, drenching, when even weekend tourists decide to get off the streets temporarily and duck into nearby shops, but we are on an errand and push past the misery of being chilled to bone—rain somehow worse than snow—when we look up and notice nothing but gray sky, yet there is something extraordinary happening, and we may begin to listen.

Walt Whitman recites a few lines from his "Song of Myself"[1]

As he walked and talked, the streets continue filling with poets, dropping as if the sudden storm has deposited them, bringing in writers from other states, distant continents, clouds carrying them over oceans and land mass until saturation with their well-crafted words, metaphors, and symbolization is so heavy that the rains fall, and writers descend, landing on their feet mostly, although a few are getting up from the pavement, their eyes looking up and out at each other, surveying cityscape, noting details of grating, minutia of reflections in water pooling on streets and sidewalks, poets keeping a mental ledger, paying careful, meticulous attention while others walk around astigmatic, talking on cell phones, cyber everything everywhere.

T. S. Eliot claimed, "April is the cruelest month" in The Waste Land [2]

It is spring, and although largely unnoticed, poets make their way to loose pages flying through air, past shops, until one hand or another grasps papers like sheet music, reading, singing, but still, the non-poets hear only the NASDAC bell and car horns, raising and lowering of delivery trucks' ramps, the ubiquitous ring tones, tablets humming, and loud voices conducting the business of business; here we have two realms simultaneously open to one another but, at the moment, unconnected, parallel and exclusive.

We live in a world increasingly dominated by technology and by demands of global business; one in which everything seems to be reduced to expediency, to wage earnings and scales that are too often more concerned with profit margins than ethics and morality. How will we alter this course? Nick Wingfield's headline to his article in the October 8, 2015, edition of the *New York Times* read, "Seattle, in Midst of Tech Boom, Tries to Keep Its Soul."[3] It would seem there are side-effects to this technology boom, and few are considering the damages.

Students now majoring in any of the humanities are becoming scarcer, a dying population, an endangered species. Humanities majors are blue whales, black rhinos, Asian elephants, and Bengal tigers. There appears to be a dialogue that suggests that the humanities are less important, less directly related to careers, and simply less. Science, technology, engineering, and mathematics are tremendously important areas of national and global life.

STEM education is a national not merely a state mandate. Yet this is not an either/or consideration. We need educated scientists, and we need humanists. The humanities are not electives in the world.

Opera singer Beverly Sills stated, "Art is the signature of civilization."[4] Former president Lyndon Johnson said, "Art is a nation's most precious heritage. For it is in our works of art that we reveal to ourselves and to others the inner vision which guides us as a nation. And where there is no vision, the people perish."[5]

Steve Jobs said, "It's in Apple's DNA that technology alone is not enough—it's technology married with liberal arts, married with the humanities, that yields us the results."[6] Consider for a moment the majors of some of the most influential and important people in your country: humanities' majors. Presidents and many members of Congress, many heads of corporations, nearly everyone in social service occupations, most of the educators you see on this stage. They once read poetry.

Listen.

Poets begin crossing over. Maybe they had crossed over regularly and were now returning, going back and forth seamlessly while others were simply less observant.

In Iran, they heard their poets loud and clear then secretly hung them. Hashem Shaabani, poet and teacher of literature, was tortured before being strung up on January 27, 2014, so his people would never forget.[7] But his people would also never forget the power of words to frame questions or take down a regime. Officially, they stated Shaabani was executed for, "waging war on God,"[8] a phrase ironically often heard in the United States as well, a condemnation of those who dare to question power.

Yet American poets may, for the most part, speak and write fairly freely. In America, however, too few read poets' words, Americans being otherwise occupied with technology, entertainment, their devices of pleasure and diversion.

Wallace Stevens can be heard reciting from his poem
"Thirteen Ways of Looking at a Blackbird"[9]

On the streets of New York, not a stock broker in sight. They have gone into offices and cubicles and left poets out in rain and ruin, poets easily mistaken for the homeless maybe because there is occasionally cross-over there. And here a poet is crossing the street and moving toward us, his eyebrows thick and unruly, leaving for distant ports, his hands a landscape of wreckage. Some move back to avoid communication or accidental exposure, surprised that he is not instantly appealing. As long as there are going to be introductions, this is not the poet they were expecting.

Robert Frost's voice can be heard in a recording of "An Old Man's Winter Night"[10]

The Night of the Murdered Poets in the summer of 1952—Stalin conducted his Pogrom in secret, trial by terror, shameless and ridiculous to the few who witnessed it and survived.[11] David Hofstein, Leib Kvitko, and Peretz Markish, among others that day and long night, suffered for their art, perhaps, but definitely for their words, tortured then executed by firing squad.[12] We could argue they were shot largely for being Jewish, not for being poets, but their symbols on the page drew attention, and fear reconfigured itself as murderer. Russia is not alone in producing and torturing her great artists and poets.

Natasha Trethewey reveals what is hidden in "Elegy for the Native Guards"[13]

We Americans have persecuted, too, but our poets are much more often ignored, and their poems unread, than their bodies imprisoned or tortured. Swinging back and forth across continents and ages like the anachrony of a nonlinear poem, we explore that distinctly American indifference. Will anyone in the United States shout, "The poets are coming; the poets are coming," a bastardization of Revere's words, "The Regulars are coming out,"[14] like some contemporary American hero?

American heroes are generally acknowledged as men of action: soldiers, policemen, snipers even. All types enacting a "just" retribution: comic book or graphic novel figures that maim in process of growing larger or stronger, quicker or more physically powerful. They are generally not poets with their "long-haired irrelevance." We hear few warnings of danger or joyous celebrations of the poets' contributions across the land.

Louise Gluck warns us in "The Wild Iris"[15]

We scarcely teach poetry in our culture anymore, teachers forced to buy into expediency, testing, business and career preparation as sole agenda, politics. And the way to capture a young person's attention is with technology, but what is poetry if it is not also sound, music, light imbued with layers of meaning? Billy Collins decided the problem with poetry is, "that it encourages the writing of more poetry."

Teaching poetry, indeed, encourages its writing but then more reading about everything eventually follows. There is always another poet to inspire, to surprise, to teach something new about language and how we think, react.

Noticed or not, poets continue to fall from the sky, each one singular as snowflakes, those hexagonal networks growing, yet without plummeting temperatures, they transform and come splashing down in a tumult of precise language and perception. Poetry is only one reason Nazis beat then shot Miklós Radnóti during the Holocaust. In their haste to destroy life, they forgot to check his jacket pocket for remaining poems, leaving "Seventh Eclogue" to speak after the young Hungarian's death.

Radnóti's words were released through their careless exit, those poems transcending the mass grave in which his remains were found, according to poet Jo Pitkin who wrote about Radnóti.[16] Reading his poem, written during his captivity, we stop at lines in which the poet's awareness of his own insignificance astonishingly becomes signifier and conduit.

Provoking and stirring the mind, poet at liminal line, Lin Zhao challenged Mao and, at the age of thirty-six, was shot down during Mao's 100 Flowers Campaign.[17] Described as "tiny and frail," Lin Zhao must have seemed a mighty foe to Mao, who it is claimed ordered her mother to pay for the bullets expended to end her daughter's life.[18] So frightened was

Mao of this young poet, he ordered her words, as well as her body, disappeared.[19]

We could travel the world and see poets persecuted. Ken Saro-Wiwa, a Nigerian poet and activist, was hung in 1995, supposedly for exposing oil interests in the region.[20] Turns out, poetry is not necessarily pretty even when it is lyrical.

W. B. Yeats quite famously exposed British brutality in his poem "Easter, 1916," in which Irish poet MacDonagh was executed along with his fellow poets, working men, and intellectuals protesting British rule of Ireland, and Yeats left us with the birth of a terrible beauty.[21]

Twenty-eight-year old Joseph Plunkett was executed with MacDonagh. Plunkett, not well known, wrote in his poem "White Waves on the Water," about doom ameliorated by dreamers,[22] expressing the sentiment that many American students believe is always the topic of this art.

How different it might be if you came in demanding poetry? It is not certain that poets are prescient; they just seem to be, and they dare to project the unimaginable, a world without them. Anna Akhmatova, a Ukrainian poet, wrote in sorrow over the persecution and deaths of her fellow poets and lover.[23] She wrote a perfect paradox about finding hope in all of that death. It is the unbearable loss that creates another poem, another voice beneath the surface.

Rita Dove makes no excuses for our lack of understanding "History"[24]

Americans write political poetry, but it is poetry in which politics more often enter through a back door. Students may ask, "Why all the sadness and death?" Because poetry can shift the continental faults in the brain—and this has been said before along those metaphoric lines—even when it is not about looking death in the face.

But poetry need not be political to jolt us, surprise, or stop us midmoment. Leonard Cohen remarked, "poetry is just the evidence of life."[25] The quotation would not be as memorable without the seemingly innocuous word "just," highlighting the fact that our words are evidence—not merely evidence—of having lived. Of course, Cohen followed that line with the equally memorable, "If your life is burning well, poetry is just the ash."[26]

Even one of the acknowledged poets of working people, Philip Levine, once stated, "I can remember feeling full of the power of a just cause and believing that power would not fail me. It failed me or I failed it. We didn't really change the way Americans lived."[27]

Of course Levine, who died recently, could not really be sure he didn't change lives. Many students and lovers of poetry would have to politely disagree with Levine. Poetry bolsters, moves minds with subtlety, suggests an alternative perception, injects new life, sets us on edge, sometimes allows someone to get up rather than lie down for good. Poetry changes "just"—to use Cohen's qualifier—one moment at a time.[28] It is also a line to remember about education.

Lawrence Ferlinghetti recently put together a little red and black book titled "Poetry as Insurgent Art," with the subtitle of the cover poem suggesting raw, blistering power through the imagery of flames.[29] Langston Hughes would have certainly nodded his head in agreement but then suggested that Ferlinghetti knew not the weight of black insurgency in America.

It seems likely Ferlinghetti and Hughes would have ultimately gotten along, with Ferlinghetti not so much having the last word as offering peace: "Poetry is eternal graffiti written in the heart of everyone,"[30] so it would appear that we should all recognize it, seek it out, go back to poetry again and again. The entrance is right there all the time, waiting for us to quiet our lives and listen closer, look beneath the literal, imagine water beneath the ground we stand on, the shift between paragraphs of breath.

Poetry has been with us in some form or other for longer than man has been writing, when he would balance his tongue on rhyme to remember history, myths, language. The Greek philosopher Plato supposedly stated, "Poetry comes nearer to vital truth than history."[31] Perhaps we are more afraid of that vital truth than a history we do not know well enough.

Without readers, however, our American poets and their words could disappear, but here they are, even if they remain invisible to many. Iranian American Azar Nafisi offers those questions in her book *The Republic of Imagination*, in which she relates an anecdote about meeting a young Iranian in a dying book store in Seattle: "'It's useless,' he said, 'your talk about books. These people are different from us—they're from another world. They don't care about books and such things.'"[32]

Perhaps access to words, to ideas—even startling ones—is too easy for Americans to take hold of even when they do not know what they are holding? If we executed our poets, we might read their works out of morbid curiosity, but that is not a suggestion any rational, moral being would seriously posit.

Maybe all of that freedom of expression has allowed such profusion of voices that we don't know where to turn; perhaps complacency breeds ignorance. Only loud, splashy things seem to make easy entrance. More likely, however, the mind is turning away from agitation toward narrow comforts.

Allen Ginsberg howls and howls in "Howl"[33]

Surprisingly, I land on my feet and look around. A former student asks me about some poems he is writing. It is important enough that his communication is in the form of instant messaging. We haven't spoken in a few years, so his note is a surprise. Reading and then reacting to his poems, I receive a quick response. I direct him to other poets whose work seems to echo in his own. "I'll have to check out more of this Larry Levis character," he writes back.

My former student is not making a living writing poetry, and it plays no part in his career plan, so why did he turn to it? He wrote that he had not thought about poetry since leaving my class, and then, suddenly, this need filled him up. He did not write a poem but a dozen poems, almost as if unable to stop. Contacting his old teacher, he sought ways to make his poems work better, not simply for himself but for others who might read them.

The problem with poetry, as Billy Collins and every practicing poet knows, is not that it causes the writing of more poetry but that it is so vitally necessary for our very souls, our state of mind, our perception of self, others, history, politic, and that "evidence of life."[34]

We allow a balding poet to touch us, surprising. Maybe we should have rethought it, but, this particular poet turns toward weather with a purpose now that didn't exist just seconds ago. It was that instant of genuine communication, that one contact transcending worlds. Another poet comes splashing in water up above her ankles as she crosses streets, walking not on water but swiftly through it, words falling from her lips.

Why these poets and their lines beneath surfaces, between spaces, between prose lines? It is worth considering these interiors of the mind, of language, of meaning, of spirit. While you are still students, you have the power to shape how we define your education, how we will educate our future as a nation on this lonely planet. As the scientist and writer Vladimir Nabokov said, "You need the passion of a scientist and the precision of a poet."[35] Surprise, it's not a contradiction.

There. Someone noticed, turned a head. Not everyone, of course. Poets continue to move outside the consciousness of many, poets' words an underground stream coursing through; yet, suddenly, we desperately want them—no, need them—to make it. Turns out, poetry requires no defense. Turns out, poetry is always with us, above as well as below consciousness, behind loud conversations, like those movements beyond silences, beyond ordinary and banal, as in Nathalie Sarraute's *Ici (Here)*.[36] Here we are, poems and the poet-scientist-mathematician-artist-historians who create them. Listen. Read. Read again. Listen. Read. Write.

We have circled back to you.

By all means, become engineers, but become metaphorical engineers, as well. Build bridges between races, between genders, between nations. Refuse false and unjust notions of hierarchy; build bridges that will allow every American access to rights guaranteed not just under law but by our common humanity.

Create your own definitions. You have the imagination to do so. And as the great scientist Albert Einstein said, "Imagination is more important than knowledge. For knowledge is limited to all we now know and understand, while imagination encircles the world, and all there ever will be to know and understand."[37]

As a lover of math and science and history and art and languages, I am only surprised he didn't write, "Imagination encircles universes."

NOTES

1. Walt Whitman, "Song of Myself," Poetry Foundation (2015), accessed February 22, 2015, http://www.poetryfoundation.org/poem/174745.
2. Eliot, *The Waste Land*.
3. Nick Wingfield, "Seattle, in the Midst of Tech Boom, Tries to Keep Its Soul," *New York Times* (October 8, 2015), accessed October 10, 2015, http://www.nytimes.com/2015/10/09/technology/seattle-in-midst-of-tech-boom-tries-to-keep-its-soul.html?_r=0.
4. Beverly Sills, BrainyQuotes.com (2001-2015), accessed February 17, 2015, http://www.brainyquote.com/quotes/quotes/b/beverlysil113151.html.
5. Lyndon Johnson, *Visionaries and Outcasts: The NEA, Congress, and the Place of the Visual Artist in America*, Michael Brenson, Books, Review, *New York Times*, accessed November 27, 2015, https://www.nytimes.com/books/first/b/brenson-outcasts.html.
6. Jonah Lehrer, "Steve Jobs, Technology Alone Is Not Enough," *New Yorker* (October 7, 2011), accessed February 17, 2015, http://www.newyorker.com/news/news-desk/steve-jobs-technology-alone-is-not-enough.
7. Saeed Kamali Dehghan, "Execution of Arab Iranian Poet Hashem Shaabani Condemned by Rights Groups," *Guardian*, Guardian News and Media Limited (February 13, 2015), accessed February 22, 2015, http://www.theguardian.com/world/2014/feb/13/iran-middleeast.
8. Dehghan, "Execution of Arab Iranian Poet Hashem Shaabani Condemned by Rights Groups."
9. Wallace Stevens, "Thirteen Ways of Looking at a Blackbird," Academy of American Poets, Poets.org, (2015), accessed February 20, 2015, https://www.poets.org/poetsorg/poem/thirteen-ways-looking-blackbird.
10. Robert Frost, "An Old Man's Winter Night," Mountain Interval, Bartleby.com, Great Books (1993–2015), accessed February 25, 2015, http://bartleby.com/119/3.html.
11. "Jewish Anti-Fascist Committee," Jewish Virtual Library, Encyclopaedia Judaica, The Gale Group (2008), accessed February 19, 2015, https://www.jewishvirtuallibrary.org/jsource/judaica/ejud_0002_0002_0_01147.html.
12. "Jewish Anti-Fascist Committee."
13. Natasha Trethewey, "Elegy for the Native Guards," Native Guard (Boston and New York: Houghton Mifflin Co., 2007).
14. Jennie Cohen, "11 Things You May Not Know about Paul Revere," History in the Headlines, History.com (April 16, 2011), accessed February 14, 2015, http://www.history.com/news/history-lists/11-things-you-may-not-know-about-paul-revere.
15. Louise Gluck, "Life, Dreams, and Reality," Poems from Celestial Music, Sohel's Blog (September 12, 2004), February 17, 2015, http://www.sohel.net/2004/09/celestial-music-15-poems-of-louise.html.
16. Jo Pitkin, "Ode to Radnóti," *Commonplace Invasions* (County Clare: Ireland, 2014), 62.
17. Ashley Sun, "Lin Zhao's Young Ghost Still Haunting China Online and Off," Tea Leaf Nation (May 16, 2011), accessed February 17, 2015, http://www.tealeafnation.com/2013/05/lin-zhaos-young-ghost-still-haunting-china-online-and-off/.
18. Ibid.
19. Ibid.
20. Ken Saro-Wiwa.
21. William Butler Yeats, "Easter, 1916," The Literature Network, (2000–2015), accessed February 25, 2015, http://www.online-literature.com/yeats/779/.

22. Joseph Mary Plunkett, "White Waves on the Water," PoemHunter.com (May 25, 2012), accessed March 2, 2015, http://www.poemhunter.com/poem/white-waves-on-the-water/.

23. Anna Akhmatova, "White Flock," World Poetry Database, accessed February 25, 2015, http://www.shigeku.com/xlib/lingshidao/waiwen/akhmatova.htm.

24. Rita Dove, "Lady Freedom among Us," University of Virginia Library, Vermont: Janus Press (November 8, 1994), accessed February 16, 2015, http://www.lib.virginia.edu/etext/fourmill/DovLady.html.

25. Leonard Cohen, BrainyQuote.com, Xplore, Inc (2015), accessed February 28, 2015, http://www.brainyquote.com/quotes/authors/l/leonard_cohen.html.

26. Leonard Cohen, BrainyQuote.

27. Hillel Italie and Scott Smith, "Poet Laureate Philip Levine Dead at 87," HuffPost Books, accessed February 15, 2015, http://www.huffingtonpost.com/2015/02/15/philip-levine-poet-laurea_n_6689146.html.

28. Leonard Cohen.

29. Lawrence Ferlinghetti, *Poetry as Insurgent Art*, San Francisco: New Directions, 2007.

30. Ibid.

31. Plato, ThinkExist.com (1999–2015), accessed October 20, 2015, http://thinkexist.com/quotation/poetry_comes_nearer_to_vital_truth_than_history/149010.html.

32. Azar Nafisi, *The Republic of Imagination: America in Three Books* (New York: Penguin Group, Viking, 2014), 1.

33. Allen Ginsberg, "Howl," Poetry Foundation (2015), accessed February 18, 2015, http://www.poetryfoundation.org/poem/179381.

34. Billy Collins, "The Trouble with Poetry: A Poem of Explanation," Edutopia (October 18, 2006), accessed February 17, 2015, http://www.edutopia.org/trouble-poetry.

35. Nabokov, *Despair*, 117.

36. Nathalie Sarraute, *Ici (Here)*, Trans. Barbara Wright, 1997 (New York: George Braziller, Inc. Gallimard Editions), 1995.

37. Albert Einstein, ThinkExist.com (1999–2015), accessed February 17, 2015, http://thinkexist.com/quotation/imagination_is_more_important_than_knowledge-for/260230.html.

TWENTY-TWO
The Answer Is the Question

The answer really is the question. Allow teachers and students to question without penalty of failing or firing. As the most inquisitive species on the planet, we are capable of designing elaborate constructions to explore; human beings are uniquely positioned to create something lasting longer than our own lives.

We are continually formulating questions about meaning, and it is in this formulation process that new ideas emerge. Perhaps if we stop looking for easy, quick fixes, we will be better able to address the complexity of the matters that plague schools and education and will be able to improve the likelihood of success for all students.

Learning begins at the position of doubt. Allow educators the freedom to design plans and curricula without punishment and encourage them to help students discover and create, find that placeholder of possibility. As a society, let us be brave enough to give our children the gift of questioning authority, question the way things are done or have been done, question the routines and the roles.

Literature and art, foreign language and music play dynamic roles in allowing students to consider the way things are. When a junior or senior in high school asks why J. D. Salinger's *The Catcher in the Rye* was banned, it is tempting to provide a pat answer, but allowing students to explore possibilities will lead to discoveries well beyond a lesson design or test.

How to we begin? Perhaps if politicians and businessmen, looking to make a killing in the "education industry," stop using hysterical and inaccurate language and broad-stroke measures toward education and public schooling, we would be able to thoughtfully assess what is working well and what needs to be addressed to improve public schooling in a lasting manner. Let us excise business terms, like stakeholders, and edu-speak from our lexicon and give the beauty of our language back to students and educators in every discipline.

Just as literature does not provide an answer but begins a journey, so, too, can education enlighten by guiding rather than penalizing students and teachers with psychological swords held over their heads. Science and literature, music and mathematics, art and history education should pose questions, taking students to places, physically, through field trips, as well as intellectually and emotionally, that they have not yet dreamed of inhabiting.

Our guide is the question, like a spiritual Fisher King, moving us between realms and past barriers. As long as we have the courage to ask and encourage questioning, students will learn and discover previously undiscovered territory.

Educators do not want to be Don Quixote, flailing at windmills, but we should and do want to engender his noble heart. We need to guide our students to seek those larger truths and reduce numbing routines, reject factory and business models, turn away from political influences or intrusions, and encourage discovery and innovation to occur simply by allowing for failures — a process that will naturally result from, but also generate, learning.

Here is a little known fact or one that is simply overlooked: excited, enthusiastic teachers and students will achieve. Students and teachers supported in risk-taking will ultimately succeed. Conversely, demeaned, demoralized teachers will fail at their challenges, and their students will struggle.

Sadly, many of the reform policies have further demoralized vast numbers of teachers who went into their profession with one goal: help children learn. One of the reasons that legislation, including Race to the Top, produced results as bleak as those laws pushing No Child Left Behind is that teachers feel beaten. It is possible that some of the directives in the new ESSA legislation will produce better results, but the problem remains: too many politicians and business interests making decisions for children.

Testing does not produce better results or, often, even accurately measure what students learn. This is something every student and teacher already knows . Perhaps if educators are given the freedom and support (in terms of hours in a day) to try new approaches and follow through with specific professional development initiatives, and if they are not continually threatened with firing over their students' test scores, we will be able to make real progress.

Perhaps if politicians stop using educators as scapegoats for sound bites and children as pawns to boost their polling numbers or bolster campaigns, we could turn to addressing the real obstacles in education that are also societal in nature. Perhaps if big money interests find another focus in order to reap exorbitant profits, we might actually be able to gradually and systematically work toward better education reform.

The tasks of reducing the powerful, outside influences, however, will be the most difficult to address. Once wealth and political power manipulators have a target in their sites, it will take the collective will and political resolve of the American electorate to stop this kind of malpractice.

The meaning of human existence—to borrow a phrase from E. O. Wilson's marvelous book—and the meaning of education reform are not about one answer or even "answers" but our continual quest to formulate and re-formulate the best possible questions. More than one species on this planet is capable of problem solving.

To verify this statement, simply look out a window and watch the seemingly ubiquitous crow tackle a problem and solve it. Only humans, however, have the gift of originating, framing, systematizing, and further developing questions; it is our especial talent and where the heart of all good education lies. Let us begin by inquiring where our children want to go before guiding them on paths to explore. Let us listen to children and allow them to raise their own questions. Let us listen to teachers and discover new avenues for connecting kids to learning.

Conceivably, someday an aging engineer will put away his high tech tools and start painting a wall, then run out to buy canvases and brushes. For all we know, the young music student will discover a way to change the sound of her instrument using a new technology she engineers. Perhaps the mathematics scholar will create an equation so perfect and advanced that she will weep before calling her colleagues to share yet another theoretical and, as yet, impractical discovery. It may be that the very well-paid engineer for a top tech corporation will stand at the edge of a bridge and choose to fly away.

As the case may be, the mid-career chemist might close his lab and return to school to become a historian and later teach others to look back, re-telling the stories of their culture, their species, and their planet to arrive at a new perspective on existence. And the STEM scholar, a well-recognized mathematician, could be found sitting alone after his wife and children have left him. At length, he takes out an old journal and is grateful he knows what to do with words.

We are neither clairvoyants nor even the paltry Madame Sosostris.[1] We cannot predict the future for our students or offer them assurances about exactly what they will face in the world or what specific jobs will definitely be available. We can, however, offer to enthusiastically guide them with clarity, well-researched plans, and provide models, teach skills, and open multiple doors in order that they may make their own choices, create their own futures, and write their own lives.

NOTE

1. T. S. Eliot, *The Waste Land*.

Appendix A

A SUGGESTED READING LIST

Bailey, Nancy E. *Misguided Education Reform: Debating the Impact on Students*. Lanham, Maryland: Rowman & Littlefield Education, 2013.

Brenson, Michael. *Visionaries and Outcasts: The NEA, Congress, and the Place of the Visual Artist in America*, first edition. New York: The New Press, 2001.

Goldstein, Dana. *The Teacher Wars: A History of America's Most Embattled Profession*. New York: Knopf Doubleday Publishing Group, 2015.

Green, Elizabeth. *Building a Better Teacher: How Teaching Works (And How to Teach It to Everyone)*. New York: W. W. Norton and Company, Inc., 2015.

Nafisi, Azar. *The Republic of Imagination: America in Three Books*. New York: Viking/Penguin Group, 2014.

Russakoff, Dale. *The Prize: Who's in Charge of America's Schools?* Houghton Mifflin Harcourt, 2015.

Shapiro, Arthur. *Education Under Siege: Frauds, Fads, Fantasies. and Fictions in Educational Reform*. Lanham, Maryland: Rowman & Littlefield Education, 2013.

Singer, Alan J. *Education Flashpoints: Fighting for America's Schools*. London: Routledge/Taylor and Francis Group, 2014.

Bibliography

Akhmatova, Anna. "Song about Song." Translation by Ilya Shambat. World Poetry Database.
Ali Manik, Julfikar and Jim Yardley. "Bangladesh Finds Gross Negligence in Factory Fire." *New York Times*. 17 December 2012. Web. 19 October 2015.
Associated Press. "Rewriting 'No Child Left Behind'—House Passes Easily." *New York Times*. 2 December 2015. Web. 12 December 2015.
Atwell, Nancie. "'World's Best Teacher' Does Not Believe in Tests and Quizzes." PBS. *News Hour*. 29 April 2015. Web. 17 October 2015.
Bajaj, Vikas. "Fatal Fire in Bangladesh Highlights the Dangers Facing Garment Workers." *New York Times*. 25 February 2012. Web. 12 September 2015.
Barnes, Robert. "Supreme Court Stops Use of Key Part of Voting Rights Act." *Washington Post*. 25 June 2013. Web. 28 September 2015.
Bipartisan Policy Center, "Former Govs: ESSA Returns Power on Education to States." 9 December 2015. Web. 12 December 12, 2015.
Bishop, Elizabeth. "In the Waiting Room." *The Complete Poems*: 1927–1979. Academy of American Poets. Poets.org. Web. 12 February 2015.
Brimelow, Peter. *The Worm in the Apple: How the Teacher Unions Are Destroying America*. New York: Harper paperbacks, 2014. Print.
Brooks, Katherine. "Meet the 2015 MacArthur Fellows." *Huffington Post*. 9 September 2015. Web. 9 September 2015.
Bush, Jeb. Fox News/Facebook. Top Ten First Tier. Debate Transcript. 6 August 2015. Web. 6 October 2015.
Carmody, Tim. "Why Education Publishing Is Big Business." Business. *Wired*. 19 January 2012. Web. 29 October 2015.
Carson, Ben, M.D., with Candy Carson. *A More Perfect Union: What We the People Can Do to Reclaim Our Constitutional Rights*. New York: Sentinel, Random House imprint, 2015. Print.
———. *One Nation: What We All Can Do to Save American's Future*. Paperback Ed. New York: Sentinel. Random House imprint, 2015. Print.
Cassidy, John. "College Calculus: What's the Real Value of Higher Education?" *New Yorker*. 7 September 2015 issue. Web. Accessed 1 September 2015.
———. "Angus Deaton: A Skeptical Optimist Wins the Economics Nobel." *New Yorker*. 12 October 2015 issue. Web. Accessed 12 October 2015.
Charette, Robert N. "The STEM Crisis Is a Myth." *IEEE Spectrum*. 30 August 2013. Web. 20 October 2015.
Cobb, Jelani. "What's Really at Stake when a School Closes?" Class Notes. Annuals of Education. *New Yorker*. Conde Nast. 1 January 2014. Web. 31 August, 2015.
Cohen, Jennie. "11 Things You May Not Know about Paul Revere." *History in the Headlines*. History.com. 18 April 2011. A&E Television Networks. 1996–2015. Web. 14 February 2015.
Cohen, Leonard. BrainyQuote.com. Xplore Inc, 2015. Web. 28 February 2015.
Colburn, David, Lynne Holt, and Lynn Leverty, Drs. "Innovation and STEM Education." The Reubin O. D. Askew Institute on Politics and Society. BEBR (Bureau of Economic and Business Research). University of Florida. Web. 10 October 2015.
Collins, Billy. "The Trouble with Poetry: A Poem of Explanation." *Edutopia*. (2006). Web. 17 February 2015. 6–7.
Covey, Stephen R. *Principle-Centered Leadership*. New York: Simon & Schuster, 1990.

Crummy, Karen and Zahira Torres. "Bloomberg, Jeb Bush among Donors to Denver, Douglas School Race," *Denver Post*. 2 November 2015. Web. 8 October 2015.
Dean, Alice M. "Symbol and Meaning in Mathematics." Skidmore College, 1995. Web. 20 November 2015.
Dehghan, Saeed Kamali. "Execution of Arab Iranian poet Hashem Shaabani Condemned by Rights Groups." *The Guardian* Online. Guardian News and Media Limited. Web. 13 February 2014.
di Stefano, Theodore F. "Why Money Chases Cheap Labor." *E-Commerce Times*. 3 February 2006. Web. 30 September 2015.
Digges, Deborah. "The Wind Blows through the Doors of My Heart." Academy of American Poets. poets.org. Web. 27 February 2015.
Doty, Mark. "Souls on Ice." Poets.org. 18 July 2000. Web. 30 September 2015.
Dove, Rita. "Lady Freedom among Us." Vermont: Janus Press. 8 November 1994. University of Virginia Library. Web. 16 February 2015.
Edison, Thomas. Edison Quotation. Goodreads Quotes. 2016. Web. 6 January 2016.
Eliot, T. S. *The Waste Land*. Bartleby.com, Great Books Online 1993–2015. Web. 27 February 2015.
"Fact Sheet: Testing Action Plan." US Department of Education. 24 October 2015. Web. 27 October 2015.
Fang, Lee. "Venture Capitalists Are Poised to 'Disrupt' Everything About the Education Market." *The Nation*. 25 September 2014. Web. 15 September 2015.
Ferlinghetti, Lawrence. *Poetry as Insurgent Art*. San Francisco: New Directions, 2007. Print.
Fldoe.org. Florida Department of Education. 2015. Web. 8 October 2015.
Frost, Robert. "An Old Man's Winter Night." *Mountain Interval*. Bartleby.com, Great Books. Web. 25 February 2015.
Gardner, John. *The Paris Review Interviews*. Vol. II. New York: Picador, 2007. Print.
Ginsberg, Allen. "Howl." Poetry Foundation 2015. Web. 18 February 2015.
Gluck, Louise. Poems from *Celestial Music*. "Life, Dreams, and Reality." Sohel's Blog. 12 September 2004. Web. 17 February 2015.
Goldstein, Dana. *The Teacher Wars: A History of America's Most Embattled Profession*. New York: Anchor Books. A Division of Penguin Random House, 2015. Print.
Gordon, Jesse. On the Issues.org. Web. 1999–2014. http://www.ontheissues.org/default.htm
Greenblatt, Stephen. "Age Is Unnecessary." Rosemond Gifford Lecture Series. 14 October 2015. Friends of the Central Library (FOCL). Syracuse New York.
———. *Will in the World: How Shakespeare Became Shakespeare*. New York: W. W. Norton and Company, 2004. Print.
Greene, Graham. "Ways of Escape." Books of the Times. Christopher Lehmann-Haupt. Review. 8 January 1981. Web. 7 December 2015.
Hardy, Quentin. "Intel to End Sponsorship of Science Talent Search." Business Day. *New York Times*. 9 September 2015. Print.
Harsin, Jill. *Colgate Scene*. Summer 2015. Print.
Hughes, Langston. "Suicide Note." PoemHunter.com. Web. 1 February 2012.
Italie, Hillel and Scott Smith. "Poet Laureate Philip Levine Dead at 87." HuffPost Books. Web. 15 February 2015.
Kasich, John. *Stand for Something: The Battle for America's Soul*. New York: Grand Central Publishing. Hachette Book Group, 2007. Print.
Kenyon, Jane. *Collected Poems*. Saint Paul: Graywolf Press, 2005. Print.
Konig, Sarah and Julie Snyder. Creators and Executive Producers. Serial. *This American Life*. October 2014. Web. 17 February 2015.
Kuhn, Harold W. and Sylvia Nasar. *The Essential John Nash*. Introduction. Princeton University Press, 2007. 8 July 2007. Web. 25 September 2015.
Lessig, Lawrence. *Republic Lost*. New York, Boston: Twelve, Hatchett Group, 2011.
Levine, Philip. "Call It Music." The Poetry Foundation. Web. 22 February, 2015.

Levis, Larry. "The Poem You Asked For." AmericanPoets. *Wrecking Crew.* 2000–2015. Web. 15 February 2015.
Lieberman, Myron. "Market Solutions to the Education Crisis." Policy Analysis. No. 75. CATO Institute. 1 July 1986. Web. 15 October 2015.
———. *Public Education: An Autopsy.* Harvard University Press, paperback, 1995.
———. *The Teacher Unions: How They Sabotage Educational Reform and Why.* Encounter Books, Perseus Books Group, 2000.
Mailer, Norman. *Harlot's Ghost.* Author's Note. New York: Random House, 2007, 1287–88.
Malone, Brian. *Education, Inc. For profit. For Kids?* Fast Forward Films. Master script transcript, 2015.
McCann, Colum. Rosamond Gifford Lecture Series. FOCL. Syracuse, NY. 15 September 2015.
McGillis, Alec. "Testing Time: Jeb Bush's Educational Experiment." The Political Scene. *New Yorker.* 26 January 2015. Web. 10 October 2015.
McQueary, Kristen. "Chicago, New Orleans, and Rebirth." *Chicago Tribune.* 13 August 2015. Web. 6 December 2015.
Menand, Louis. "What's It All About?" Bowdoin College. Bowdoin.edu. 22 October 2010. Web. 28 October 2015.
Mencimer, Stephanie. "Jeb Bush's Cyber Attack on Public Schools." *Mother Jones.* Nov–Dec 2001. Web. 26 October 2015.
Merwin, W. S. "The Asians Dying." *The Second Four Books of Poems.* Copper Canyon Press, 1993. Print.
Moran, Lawrence A. "The Problem with STEM." University of Toronto. Sandwalk. Blogspot, 2011. Web. 27 October 2015.
Nabokov, Vladimir. *Despair.* New York: Vantage International Ed., Division of Random House, 1989. Print.
Nafisi, Azar. *The Republic of Imagination: America in Three Books.* New York: Viking, Penguin Group, 2014. Print.
Obama, Barack, President of the United States of America. "An Open Letter to America's Parents and Teachers: Let's Make Our Testing Smarter." The Blog, HuffPost Politics. *Huffington Post.* 28 October 2015. Web. 28 October 2015.
O'Gara, Gwynn. "Winter." *Winter at Green Haven.* Santa Rosa, California: Word Temple Press, 2008. Print.
Ogawa, Yoko. *The Housekeeper and the Professor.* New York: Picador Edition, translation, 2009.
O'Hara, Frank. "Homosexuality." PoemHunter.com.13 January 2003. Web. 20 February 2015.
Owens, Jeff, II. Summative LAT Essay. College Prep English. ESM Central High School. May 2015.
Pastan, Linda. "Emily Dickinson." PoemHunter.com. 13 January 2003. Web. 15 February 2015.
Pitkin, Jo. *Commonplace Invasions.* Ireland: Salmon Poetry 2014. Print.
Plath, Sylvia. "Fever 103" Poetry Foundation 2015. Web. 17 February 2015.
Plato. ThinkExist.com. 1999–2025. Web. 22 February 2015.
Plunkett, Joseph Mary. "White Waves on the Water." PoemHunter.com. 2 February 2015, Web. 2 March 2015.
Proteacher.net. #4. 23 April 2006. Web. 7 October 2015.
Reich, Rob. "School Reform Is Failing America's Children: To Hell with Good Intentions." *Boston Review.* 5 November 2015. Web. 7 December 2015.
Ricotti, Joseph A. "Education Reform Is Basically an Anti-Teacher Movement." *Connecticut Post.* CTpost.com. Hearst Media Services. 2 September 2011. Web. 28 October 2015.
Roethke, Theodore. *The Far Field: Last Poems.* Anchor Books Edition. Garden City, New York: Doubleday and Company, 1971. Print.

Rumens, Carol. "Tichborne's Elegy by Chidiock Tichborne." *Guardian*. Guardian News and Media Limited. 26 November 2012. Web. 20 February 2015.

Sarraute, Nathalie. *Here*. Translated by Barbara Wright. New York: George Braziller, Inc., 1997. Copyright Gallimard Editions, 1995. Print.

Satlin, Alana Horowitz. "John Nash Dead: 'A Beautiful Mind' Mathematician Killed in Car Accident." *Huffington Post*. HuffingtonPost.com, Inc. 24 May 2015. Web. 26 October 2015.

SETDA. 2015. Web. 9 October 2015.

Sherburn, George. "The Early Popularity of Milton's Minor Poems." JSTOR. Chicago Journals. *Modern Philology*. Vol. 17, no 5 (Sept. 1919). Web. 22 February 2015.

Sherman, Ted and Myles Ma. "Famed 'A Beautiful Mind' Mathematician John Nash, Wife, Killed in N.J. Turnpike Crash." *NJ Advance Media* for NJ.com. 28 May 2015. Web. 2 October 2015.

Shneer, David. Jewish Virtual Library. *Encyclopaedia Judaica*. The Gale Group, 2008. Web. 19 February 2015.

Singer, Alan. "Despite Big Problems Charters Attract Hedge Fund Support and Presidential Candidates Hungry for Dollars." *Huffington Post*. HuffPost.com. 1 October 2015. Web. 28 October 2015.

STEMSchool.com. 9 December 2012. Web. 27 November 2015.

Stevens, Justice John Paul. Dissenting opinion in the Citizens United ruling. Legal Information Institute. Cornell University Law School. *Citizens United v. Federal Election Comm'n* (No. 08-205). 21 January 2010. Web. 6 October 2012.

Stevens, Wallace. "Thirteen Ways of Looking at a Blackbird." Academy of American Poets. Poets.org. Web. 20 February 2015.

Stix, Gary. "Lifting the Curse of Alzheimer's." *Scientific American*. Vol. 312, no. 5 (May 2015).

Strauss, Valeria. "Jeb Bush Bashes Traditional Public Schools (Again)." *Washington Post*. 10 May 2014. Web. 8 October 2015.

Sullivan, Maureen. "Rand Paul on Education: 5 Things the Presidential Candidate Wants You to Know." *Forbes*. Web. 7 April 2015.

Sun, Ashley. "Lin Zhao's Young Ghost Still Haunting China Online and Off." *TeaLeafNation*. Web. 17 February 2015.

Tannenbaum, Melanie. "'But I Didn't Mean It!' Why It's So Hard to Prioritize Impacts over Intents." *Scientific American*. 14 October 2013. Web. 14 September 2015.

Taylor, Kate. "Cuomo's Education Agenda Sets Battle Lines with Teachers' Unions." *New York Times*. 20 January 2015. Web. 12 October 2015.

Tichborne, Chidiock. *Wikipedia*. 19 October 2014. Web. 20 February 2015.

TheSKIMM. *Huffington Post*. 7 October 2015. Web. 8 October 2015.

Thompson, Derek. "A World without Work." *Atlantic*. July/August 2015. Vol. 316, no. 1. Washington, DC (51–61). Print.

Trethewey, Natasha. "Elegy for the Native Guards." *Native Guard*, Boston and New York: Houghton Mifflin Co. First Mariner Books edition, 2007. Print.

"[Twenty-four] 24 New Teacher Quality Partnership Grants Totaling More Than $35 Million Awarded to Recruit, Train and Support More Science, Technology, Engineering and Math Teachers." US Department of Education. Press Office, http://www.ed.gov/news. Web. 28 September 2015.

Van Straaten, Laura. "The New Digital Art Service That Puts Color First." Art Matters. *New York Times*. 19 October 2015. Web. 10 October 2015.

Walker, Jade. "3 Win the 2015 Nobel Prize in Chemistry for Studies in DNA Repair." *Huffington Post*. AOL Tech. 7 October 2015. Web. 8 October 2015.

Wallis, Claudia. "No Child Left Behind: Doomed to Fail?" Kennedy's Top Ten Legislative Battles, *Time* (8 June 2008), accessed 1 January 2016.

Whitman, Walt. "Song of Myself." Poetry Foundation. 2015. Web. 22 February 2015.

Wilczek, Frank. *A Beautiful Question: Finding Nature's Deep Design*. New York: Penguin Press, 2015. Print.

Wilson, Edward O. *The Meaning of Human Existence*. New York: Liveright Publications Corporation, Division of W. W. Norton and Co., paperback edition, 2015. Print.
Wingfield, Nick. "Seattle, in Midst of Tech Boom, Tries to Keep Its Soul." *New York Times*. 8 October 2015. Web. 10 October 2015.
Yeats, William Butler. "Easter, 1916." The Literature Network. Jalic Inc. 2000. Web. 25 February 2015.

About the Author of the Foreword

Nationally honored and recognized educator **Sally B. Mitchell** began her teaching career in 1982 and has taught chemistry, Syracuse University Project Advance (SUPA) chemistry and forensics, biology, physics, and mathematics. Serving in the Office of Science for the US Department of Energy, Mitchell is an Albert Einstein Distinguished Educator Fellow for 2015–2016. She also currently holds the position of the American Chemical Society Expert in STEM and is serving on the governance board of the newly formed American Association of Chemistry Teachers as a special consultant. A New York State designated master teacher in science, Mitchell has been recognized as an outstanding teacher by the Technology Alliance of Central New York, among others. Through initiatives such as Chemagination, ACS's Chemists Celebrate Earth Day, Science Olympiad, and National Chemistry Week, she exposes students to experiences beyond the classroom. She holds a dual bachelor of science degree in chemistry and biology and a master's in science from Syracuse University.

In addition, Mitchell has created and produced an award-winning video entitled "Everyday Chemistry." Sally B. Mitchell was the recipient of the James Bryant Conant Award for outstanding teaching in high school chemistry in 2009. She is published in the *Journal of Chemical Education*.

About the Author

Nancy Avery Dafoe is a published writer and educator living in Central New York. A New York State English Council Teacher of Excellence, Dafoe has taught a wide variety of courses in English at the high school and college level for many years. She is a state conference and Teacher Center presenter on a variety of topics.

Dafoe has also written books for educators and preservice teachers on writing instruction. Her books include *Breaking Open the Box: A Guide for Creative Techniques to Improve Academic Writing and Generate Critical Thinking*, and a companion book for classroom use, *Writing Creatively: A Guided Journal to Using Literary Devices*, published by Rowman & Littlefield Education in 2013 and 2014, respectively.

Her cross-genre memoir and poetry book on dealing with Alzheimer's, *An Iceberg in Paradise: A Passage through Alzheimer's* (2015). Excerpts from Dafoe's fiction are included in the anthology *Lost Orchard*, edited by Jo Pitkin (2014). Dafoe's essays, fiction, book reviews, and poetry have won numerous awards and appeared in a number of literary magazines and publications.

www.ingramcontent.com/pod-product-compliance
Lightning Source LLC
Chambersburg PA
CBHW021845220426

43663CB00005B/407

* 9 781475 828320 *